The Emotional Imperative

How Emotions Rule Our Lives

The Emotional Imperative

How Emotions Rule Our Lives

D. M. Miller

ISBN 1453601481

EAN-13   9781453601488.

Concerning the cover illustration:

Illustrated on the front cover is an inukshuk, a cairn of stones in the form of a human figure. Structures of this type are used by the natives in the arctic to direct stampeding herds of caribou towards hunters, and to indicate the presence of encampments or caches. These landmarks are erected by the Inuit, a resourceful people driven by the fires of genocide to the very fringes of the inhabitable world. Here they eke out a bare subsistence in a land shunned by more aggressive races. Inukshuks are frequently the only evidence that the land is occupied, and, rising in stark contrast to the barren polar landscape, serve as a monument to the tenacity of the survivors - and as a poignant memorial to the victims of mankind's genocidal struggle for supremacy!

CONTENTS

PROLOGUE

Why do we rush from a burning building?

Most would consider this action to be taken in response to the powerful emotion - **fear**. Others would argue that, as man is a rational animal, his response must be motivated by reason. This seems obvious since it requires the intellect to assess the danger, plan a means of escape and make us aware that we are in danger of being injured or killed.

But why should it matter if we were to be injured or killed?

The answer to this is obvious to us all - because we don't want to die, or because we wish to live! Both **want** and **wish** are terms steeped in emotion and without logical progenitors! We consider them to be obvious and indisputable.

It is evident, then, that the actions we take in response to a threat are ultimately driven by an **emotional imperative** - not by reason! This is true also of all the stronger feelings we usually term "**emotions,**" such as love, hate, anger, etc. - which must, therefore, be inherent in us all.

The proposition advanced in this book is that - not only do the more powerful drives we experience cause us to take specific actions - but that **all the actions we take are in response to emotional imperatives - urges or drives that are instilled in us by genes whose propagation depends on the contribution made to our biological success by the behavior these urges or drives inspire in us**.

A corollary to this proposition is that, while our intellect may set interim goals, **all our ultimate goals are set by our emotions - none by our intellect**!

This proposition also provides us with a definition of the term **behavior** as **all the actions taken by animals in response to the emotional urges to which they are subject.**

It is my intention in this work to show that by accepting this proposal we may answer such questions as - what is the origin of altruism - of nationalism and modern nation-states - of humor - of the generation gap - of morality - of male dominance - of religion - and, in fact, of all the other behavioral characteristics possessed by our species?

We begin by adopting the view of most scientists that life was generated on earth by natural forces some three to three and a half billion years ago. We will not be concerned with this aspect of human origins, however, but rather with the forces that have shaped the specific nature of our species. In particular I will attempt to show that the behaviors we exhibit are fashioned by **emotional imperatives - urges that have, themselves, been selected and retained by natural forces because they have promoted, and continue to promote, the welfare - not only of the species itself - but rather, of each of the individual members of the species.** This is important since natural selection of fit individuals themselves - and not the species as a whole - is the basic mechanism that has directed the evolutionary process.

Furthermore, it will be argued, that qualities such as 'altruism' and 'goodness', in combination with other qualities, have, in the past, increased the fitness of individuals of the human species.

To develop this argument, we will first consider the mechanism of evolution in its broadest sense, and then attempt to show in more specific terms how natural selection - the driving force of evolution - might have been responsible for shaping the characteristics possessed by modern humans. Speculation on the processes occurring in the mind will follow, during which we will distinguish between emotional and rational functions. Finally I hope to convince you that the social, moral, and religious aspects of our species are a natural consequence of the evolutionary processes as outlined.

Perhaps, however, I should first justify my proposed use of the theory of evolution to explain human nature, especially since it has recently come under criticism as being little better than the **creationists' contention.** My preference for the former over the latter arises from my view of scientific theories in general. The prime purpose of any **theory** is to coordinate facts; the more facts a theory coordinates, or 'explains', the more useful it is and the more credibility it enjoys.

The work of the scientist is first to collect data or facts. Next a proposal or **hypothesis** is advanced to explain how the observations, or facts, might be related to each other. A useful hypothesis will then suggest other experiments or means of obtaining further facts, which may or may not correspond to the predictions of the hypothesis. If the hypothesis is successful in this test, it is then elaborated into a **theory**, whose purpose is to explain the observations. Further facts are then sought to test the theory.

A **law**, on the other hand, is considered to be absolute. It is given that status only because, as my professor of thermodynamics informed his students: "The opposite has never been observed to occur." As an example: we are all aware that an iron bar heated at one end will, in time, distribute this heat equally to all its parts. This is predicted by the **laws of thermodynamics**, which can be considered to be laws only so long as there is no *well-authenticated* case of the opposite occurring (such as an iron bar spontaneously becoming hotter at one end than the other). But even if this is so in our limited experience, there is no assurance that under certain improbable conditions - or at other times or places in the universe - the opposite could not, or has not occurred. We see, then, that **absolute**

knowledge does not exist and therefore, that it is impossible to prove any theory - or for that matter, any 'law' - absolutely.

Hypotheses, theories and laws are, in fact, only constructs fashioned by the human mind in its attempt to organize and store the myriad facts that daily experience presents it with. There is nothing absolute about them, nor is there any evidence that they exist outside our minds. They differ from each other only in the degree of confidence with which we regard them, and this confidence is, as I have already stated, directly proportional to the number and variety of facts that they are able to correlate.

Our knowledge concerning the development of life on earth is enormous, and evolutionary theory has been exceedingly effective in making this process comprehensible to us. The theory of evolution is not fixed or immutable, however, but like a living thing is itself evolving and will continue to evolve and to gain power as our knowledge grows.

Creationism denies the vast spectacle of a flowering earth, preferring instead to view the origin of life as the sudden appearance of essentially immutable life forms, whose individual designs result from the whims of a superior intelligence (the creator). It provides no reasons for the variety of life forms, stating only that things are the way they are because they were *created* that way. We are given no reason for the development of the long neck of the giraffe, or why an insect has six legs, or why the hemoglobin molecule varies in structure the way it does throughout the animal world. It cannot qualify as an hypothesis (much less a theory) since it coordinates few, if any, facts - such as why the creator made things the way they are - and gives no comprehensive picture of the broad panorama of living things. In my opinion the creationist's contention is intellectually vapid and unqualified for the assignment we have set ourselves here and will therefore not be considered further in the following discussion.

A more intriguing subject than the creationists' contention itself, however, would be to study the reason such irrationalities arise in the first place, and in this regard, I propose to show that those individuals advancing such so-called theories, do so in response to urges instilled by genes which are themselves an inevitable product of the mechanism of natural selection - *the very mechanism that these individuals seek to refute!*

The main thesis advanced in this work, is that human nature - including moral behavior - is the direct result of the action of natural selection. All the longings - the impulses - the urges - the goals that modern humans exhibit, are those that have resisted the ravages of natural selection, the ultimate judge of who is to survive, and cruel master who has decreed that the heritage of failure is oblivion!

Thus the belief in a personal God - although it is probably no more than a lie told by our genes - has led to behavior that increased our ability to survive and assured the propagation of those genes leading some of us to formulate such beliefs!

A more appropriate title for this work might have been *Speculations.* Let us not denigrate speculation, however, which although imprecise, is the very sap of the tree of knowledge, nourishing the buds of empiricism and extending the branches of knowledge in previously unforeseen directions.

Should you, the reader, find the propositions contained herein to be absurd or repugnant, two options are open to you. You can close the book now with the confidence that - since your faith is unassailable - nothing would be gained by considering such ridiculous proposals further. On the other hand, if you wish to test your faith, or if your curiosity propels you, let us, in the following pages, assess the credibility of this thesis - and what may be more interesting, determine the reasons that many of us find its propositions not only repugnant, but dangerous and frightening as well!

It is not my only purpose in this work to be an iconoclast, but rather, more importantly, to assess honestly who we are and what we are, so that we may seek progress without illusion. Unfortunately, to do so requires that we dispense with many of the emotional buffers we have fashioned in an attempt to ease our vital passage!

Be aware, then - before proceeding - that

> *Our purpose strives for truth - not to reassure.*
> *If you are seeking comfort, you will not find it here!*

Many of the terms used in this work are defined during the course of the discussion in an effort to stipulate - as precisely as possible - the sense in which they are employed here. Readers who wish to review these definitions at any time may do so by consulting the index at the end of the book, where the locations of the definitions in the text are listed.

CHAPTER ONE

THE MECHANISM OF THE EVOLUTIONARY PROCESS

May the might of destiny grant me
The supreme ecstasy of earthly joy
To see, when I arise from the tomb,
My art thriving peacefully
Among those who come after me.
Gregor Mendel

Charles Darwin first published the complete form of his theory - that complex life forms evolved from simpler equivalents - in 1859. It was based on four main observations:

- Most organisms tend to produce offspring that are more numerous than their parents, leading to the expectation that their numbers should increase geometrically.

- In spite of this, the population sizes of most organisms remain constant over long periods.

- The attributes of an organism are inherited from its parents. The offspring of sexually reproducing pairs derive part of their attributes from each parent and therefore differ from both parents.

- All biological species show variations in the attributes that characterize that species.

From the first two facts it is clear that only a few individuals of each generation can themselves reproduce. Thus the members of a biological species must, not only battle great odds to reach maturity, but face further competition with their fellows to reproduce. These two conflicts Darwin termed the **struggle for survival.**

From the second two assumptions he concluded that only the attributes possessed by individuals who were successful - first of all in surviving to maturity, and secondly, in reproducing - would be passed on to following generations, while qualities detrimental to the functioning of the individual would eventually be eliminated. This process, which Darwin termed **natural selection** would, he claimed, bring about a gradual change in the overall characteristics of a species. The nature of the changes, according to this view, would depend on the challenges faced by an organism, which in turn, would be dictated by its environment. Thus the history of evolution would differ in accordance with differences in geographical location and ultimately result in the formation of new species.

Critics of natural selection objected to the theory since it appeared to be destructive rather than synthetic; thus one might accept that undesirable characteristics could be eliminated from a species by natural selection, but it was not obvious how these mechanisms could lead to the formation of new species. Darwin, however, was ignorant of the work of Mendel, as were most of his contemporaries. They did not know, for example, of the existence of genes - nor of the occurrence of **mutation**, which could introduce spontaneous changes into genetic material.

Let us now consider these important aspects of biology.

The Experiments of Gregor Mendel

The only existing record of the experiments of the Augustinian monk, Gregor Mendel, on the hybridization of peas, appeared in a single paper published in an obscure nature journal in 1865 (a mere seven years after Darwin published his complete theory). This work was ignored until 1900 when it was brought to the attention of workers in the field and reinterpreted it in terms of newer information in cytology.

The most important aspect of Mendel's work is that it showed that characteristics were inherited in a quantized form, rather than in a blended form, as assumed by the naturalists of Darwin's day.

Mendel demonstrated the particulate nature of inheritance by showing that a hybrid, or heterozygote, transmits to each of its sex cells only one factor - not both - of the pair it had itself received from its parents.

Thus, for example, two plants, one bearing white and one bearing red flowers, would not produce offspring all of whose flowers were a blend of the two colors (i.e. pink, in this case), but rather, each offspring would develop flowers of just one or other of the two colors. Furthermore, according to Mendelian laws, there would be a definite and predictable ratio between the numbers of offspring bearing each color of flower. The results of Mendel's experiments cannot be explained by any mechanism that does not assume the existence of discrete units of transfer of **characteristics** or **traits** from parent to offspring and it is these units of inheritance that we refer to as **genes**.

The modern interpretation of these experiments is that the gene for flower color has two variants - or **alleles** - one specifying red flowers and the other specifying white flowers. Mendel also showed that of the two alleles, one was **dominant** and the other **recessive**. When both are present in an offspring, only the dominant allele is expressed - thus, for the recessive characteristic to appear, the carrier must receive one copy of the recessive gene from each parent.

Size - a Different Type of Characteristic

Now let us consider another trait found in all animals - their relative size. We have observed that larger parents tend to have larger offspring, while smaller animals have smaller issue. We conclude from this, that size, although affected by environmental factors, is under genetic control. This has been confirmed through the breeding of domesticated animals, where by selecting breeding pairs we can influence various characteristics of the offspring, including their size. We note this also in humans, whose family members show similarities in such traits as height relative to the general population.

On the other hand, we do not find that this trait resembles that of color in Mendel's plants, since it does not have only two outcomes - which in this case would be either short or tall. Instead, we find a range of heights between very short and very tall. In fact, when we plot the height of healthy human males of a similar age - for which there is an enormous amount of data (mostly from the military) - against the number of men within a given height range, the result is a bar graph of the type shown in Figure 1A.

A similar bar graph of the data from Mendel's flower color experiment could be made. To do this, it would be necessary to quantify the data by extracting and determining the amount of red pigment in the petals of the flowers of each of the plants derived from the breeding of two hybrids. Plotting the amount of this pigment (per gram of petals) taken from each plant, against the number of plants whose flowers have this amount would result in a bar graph of the type shown in Figure 1B.

In both these plots, the horizontal axis (**x-axis**) is the magnitude, or the **intensity**, of the characteristic being measured. For the height-of-men graph, the intensity is the height itself, while for the flower data, it is the amount of pigment present in the petals. The vertical axis (**y-axis**), on the other hand, has the same units in both graphs, being the fraction of the total population displaying the corresponding intensity. As we can see, the plot of the flower data has a totally different form to that of the height data, consisting of only two bars (whose widths depend on the accuracy of the analytical method), with that representing the highly pigmented (red) population having approximately three times the height of the non-pigmented (white) flowers.

How can we account for this difference between two presumably inherited traits?

The Normal Distribution Curve

To answer this question, let us return to the height data. It has long been known that these data can be fitted approximately by what is known as a **normal distribution curve** - such as the one plotted in Figure 1A. This **bell-shaped curve,** as it is sometimes called (because of its shape), was originally found to predict the errors in astronomical and other physical measurements very closely and is therefore also referred to as an **error curve**. An equation describing normal distribution quantitatively,

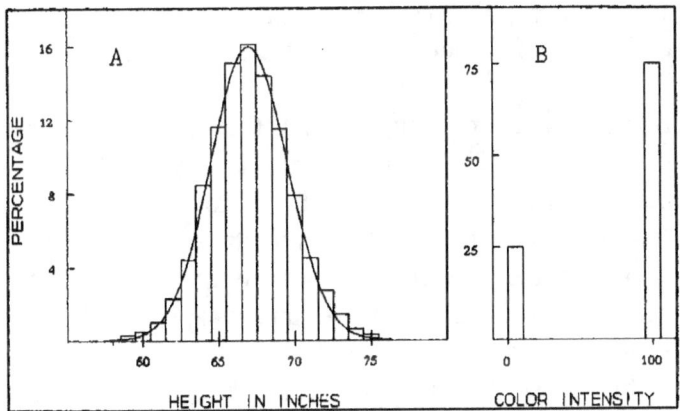

Figure 1A. *Bar Graph* - The height of the bars is proportional to the percentage of a population of men whose heights are between those indicated by the vertical lines defining each bar - that is, within each specified one inch interval.

Smooth Curve - A normal distribution curve fitted to the height data.   Average = 67 inches, standard deviation = 2.5 inches.

Figure 1B. Hypothetical bar graph for the intensity of color in pea flowers.

was derived over two hundred years ago using the laws of chance as its basis. This equation appears to be successful in describing quantitatively most of the observations of phenomena showing variations in the quantity being measured, since it predicts the probability of finding an error (or deviation from the average) of a given magnitude in any measurement. As a corollary, then, we are probably safe in assuming that any data which fit the equation must be subject to chance variations.

We can illustrate how chance plays a part in such measurements by considering the success of a marksman attempting to strike a target or bull's eye. The reasons each shot is not perfect, are many. For example, there may be differences in the currents or temperature of the air through which the bullet is passing; there may be a gradual build-up of carbon inside the rifle barrel or changes in the temperature of the barrel; the amount of propellent in each cartridge or the symmetry of the bullet may vary from cartridge to cartridge; there may be spurious discharges in the hundreds of nerves and synapses feeding the muscles which steady the marksman's aim and cause him to squeeze the trigger; there may be variations in the marksman's judgement of his aim and the compensations he makes consciously or unconsciously, for the errors in previous shots. No doubt there are many other factors affecting accuracy, so that no two shots are unlikely to be the same.

Now let us consider a hypothetical situation in which all these errors are minimized - as for example, by using an indoor range, clamping the rifle, selecting the ammunition carefully etc. - with the result that all the bullets strike a very small area within the bull's-eye. Suppose, however, that we were to locate a fan on the left side of the range which, when operating, directed a current of air across the bullet's trajectory causing it to be deflected to the right. The result would be that when the fan was not operating, all shots would enter the target very close to its centre, forming a tight grouping of hits at this point. When the fan was operational, however, all shots would be deflected by the same amount, forming a second tight grouping at some distance to the right of the first. Suppose further that the fan was controlled by an operator, who, before each shot, turned the fan on or off in accordance with the results of the toss of two coins - 'on' when at least one of the coins came up 'heads', or 'off' when neither did. Plotting the number of hits for a large number of shots as a function of their distance from the target center would result in a curve similar to Figure 1B, in that it would have two peaks for which the height of the one on the right would be approximately three times that of the one on the left. The reason for the factor of three is that, of the four equally possible outcomes (two heads, two tails, the first a head and second a tail, the first a tail and the second a head), three cause the fan to operate and to deflect the bullet.

This experiment is similar to Mendel's flower collor measurements, since in both cases, the decision as to which of two possible outcomes is realized, is determined by a single random event. In the flower experiment this event is the genetic contribution made by each of the two parents at conception, while for the target example the outcome is contingent on the toss of two coins. In both cases the outcome is a product of pure chance.

It is possible, however, that the outcome could be decided by many events. For the target example, this would be the case if we were to replace the single large fan by many small fans, each independently controlled by its own operator, who would decide its operational status in the usual fashion prior to each shot. The intensity of the deflection during each shot would then be proportional to the number of fans in the 'on' position, which itself is a variable quantity. For a large number of shots, plotting the fraction of the total number of shots having a specific deflection, against that deflection, as before, would provide a plot, not like 1B, but rather, like 1A - a normal distribution curve.

From this we may conclude that such a curve is generated by a **multi-factorial process** - one in which a number of factors influence the outcome. In the case of the target example, these factors are the coin tosses and so it is a reasonable assumption to assign a similar role to the gene make-up of each individual in the height-of-men measurements. This observation allows us to reach an important conclusion - that *any plot of a variable quantity displaying a bell-shaped distribution is likely to be the product of a multi-factorial process.*

The accuracy with which any data fit the theoretical curve, increases with the number of measurements made. Thus, after an infinite number of measurements, the **mean value** of the heights will equal the numeric **average** of all the measurements, and since the curve is symmetrical, the average coincides with the peak of the curve, *the height most commonly found in the male population.*

The heights of most individuals deviate from the average, however, and the shape of the curve tells us that smaller **deviations** are far more common than larger deviations. Furthermore, these deviations are just as likely to be positive as negative. The largest deviations occur in the **tails** (or ends) of the curve, where the frequencies approach zero.

The most striking aspect of the height data is the accuracy with which they fit the calculated curve, duplicating its smoothness and lack of imposed peaks or valleys. This implies that of all the factors contributing to the height of an individual, none is as outstanding as are those in the flower data. Furthermore, we may conclude, that there must be a large number of such factors to produce such a smooth curve. Assuming that - as in the case of the flower data - the intensity is a product of genetic action, height must result from the influence of, not one gene, but of many.

Intelligence

Intelligence may be defined as *the ability to make decisions to act in ways that contribute to the success of the individual.*

This trait, as it functions in humans, is probably the most powerful survival mechanism to have evolved in any species - yet its exact definition still eludes us! This is due, no doubt, to its extreme complexity, which results from the large number of components, or aspects, of which it consists. The normal distribution curve has been extensively employed in these studies, confirming the random and complex nature of this trait.

A variety of attempts to enumerate all the various facets of intelligence have been made. These enumerations have included such terms as thinking, reasoning, memory, learning, perception, decision-making, adaptability, originality, productiveness, understanding, judgment, cleverness, common sense, arithmetic ability, inductive reasoning, abstract thinking, spatial visualization, the ability to understand word meanings - and many more.

Despite the lack of a universally accepted definition for this trait, many attempts to measure it quantitatively have been made. The results of these measurements in various populations, when reduced to a number termed I. Q. (for **intelligence quotient**), and plotted appropriately, have been found to correspond roughly to a bell-shaped curve, showing that our intelligence is probably polygenetic in origin. In fact it is likely that many of its components themselves are polygenetic, and furthermore, it appears that each of us has a unique profile of these components, with strengths in some areas and weaknesses in others. We may say, then, that the **quality** of this trait varies from person to person.

It is generally agreed, however, that I. Q. tests do not measure wisdom, creativity, common sense, social skills, or practical knowledge - abilities that allow people to adapt to everyday problems. It is also agreed that the origins of intelligence are not entirely genetic, but that the environment - particularly past experience - plays a major role in determining the strength of each of our mental capabilities. Perhaps this is so because some of these capabilities, by their very nature, appear to be enhanced, or strengthened, by training.

The Subjective Nature of Traits

One of the reasons that there are several factors involved in many traits is our definition of what we consider to be traits or characteristics. We are immediately conscious of a person's height on our first meeting and are therefore prepared to designate height as one of the characteristics of that person. On the other hand, we certainly are not aware of that same person's blood type, which is also under genetic control. Nor do we all agree on what constitutes goodness and on the degree to which others possess this trait, since each of us makes such decisions based on our individual biases, experience and knowledge. This illustrates the subjective nature of our definition of a trait.

But just because our definition of a trait is subjective does not mean that we should reject the trait itself as a factor in evolution. On the contrary, the size of organisms (and as we shall see, the degree of goodness in humans as well) can be decisive in determining their chances for survival and in fact the average size of every species has been determined mainly by selective pressures. If a certain size is of advantage to an animal, then individuals of that size will be more successful in surviving and reproducing than other individuals, causing the genes specifying this size, to proliferate.

Size is only one of the enormous number of traits that define the individual and contribute to its ability to survive. As a result of this large number of traits, there is considerable variability in the offspring of even a single mating pair of individuals, and even more variability when considering a population of the members of a single species. This variability is due mainly to the fact that each individual has so many characteristics and can therefore differ from other members of its species in so many ways.

Polygenetic Traits

The deviations from the average in the height-of-men data are not due to errors in the measurements - since these are much less than the size of the deviations observed - but rather, are due to other factors that affect the heights themselves. The whole point of this approach is to illustrate, by analogy, that traits in organisms may not always be controlled by a single gene, but that in fact many traits are **polygenetic - the product of the activity of a large number of genes and gene products.**

In the case of the height of individuals, for example, there will be genes controlling the lengths of the bones of the legs and vertebrae as well as the biochemical synthesis and time of activity of the growth hormone and the sites in the tissues with which the hormone combines to produce its effect - to name but a few. These effects are, of course, independent of non-genetic or environmental factors, such as malnutrition and sickness, which will also produce variations in height, but are not of interest here.

The intensity of a trait in each individual will be the sum of the intensities specified by each of the genes contributing to this feature. Not all the genes that may contribute to a polygenetic trait will do so with the same intensity in every individual, but rather, will vary from individual to individual *according to the laws of chance*, accounting for the scatter that characterizes this trait and the fact that its frequency distribution approaches that of a normal distribution.

These conclusions are only valid provided the heights measured are truly random, or unbiased.

Thus we may conclude that since any plot of a variable quantity approximating a normal distribution is likely to be the product of a multi-factorial process, it follows that *any biological characteristic whose intensity approximates a normal distribution in a population is likely to be polygenetic in origin.* A corollary of this is that *any polygenetic trait will approximate a normal distribution in the magnitude of the intensities with which it is expressed within the population.*

Selection of Mono- and Polygenetic Traits

When selection is specific for a single gene, as it is in Mendel's experiments, the effect on the individual is all or nothing; that is, either the plant's flowers are one color or another. Selection for one color in this case alters the gene frequency for the various colors in the gene pool of the population as a whole. For a polygenetic trait, on the other hand, the intensity of a trait is altered, not only in the population, but in each individual as well. If we were to plot the intensity-frequency curve for this trait in a population under selective pressure over time, we would observe a drift in the average intensity for this characteristic toward higher or lower values - or, in more general terms, a shift of the entire bell-shaped curve along the intensity axis in one direction or another. We shall consider this feature of the selective process more fully below.

Gene Complexes - Genes Selected in Common

It is probable that many, if not most, of the characteristics of an organism that are selected during evolution, are polygenetic; that is, they are traits that are the product of not one gene, but result from the interaction of a number - possibly even a large number - of genes and gene products. I shall refer to all the genes that have any effect on a characteristic as a **gene complex**. The complete **genetic complement** of an individual is usually termed the **genotype** and the total of all genes present in a population of interbreeding organisms is usually referred to as a **gene pool** or **genome** - the sum of all genotypes in the species. *I am not suggesting that the genes in a gene complex are necessarily located together on the same chromosome - only that if they all contribute to a trait, they will all be selected for or against as the trait itself is.*

The reason I refer to the complete genetic make-up of an individual as its **gene complement** is that I believe that most genes operate within the context of all the other genes possessed by the individual. Furthermore, it is because few genes act independently of their fellow genes, that the traits exhibited within a gene pool have such variability and why the intensity with which they are expressed follows a normal distribution.

Multi-Functional Genes

In many cases, a gene may have a function in specifying two entirely separate attributes. As an example, it is possible for a flower pigment to have anti-fungal properties. Would we then say, if this were the case, that the gene producing this pigment is 'for' a certain color of flower, or 'for' protection of the plant against fungal infections? We could argue that of all the qualities that a gene specifies, the one that is most critical to the survival of its carrier is the one we should consider to be its primary function. However, the importance of a trait to an organism can depend on the environmental conditions. Thus in wet years, when fungal infections are high, the anti-fungal aspect of the derivative of the gene for flower color will cause it to be selected, whereas other years, its attractiveness to pollinators may be its most important quality.

The Functional Optimum

As we have seen, when considering a genetic characteristic, there are two quantitative dimensions of interest - the intensity with which it is expressed in each individual and the frequency with which each individual intensity occurs in the population. This is the reason that, when we plot such data, we do so using a two-dimensional plot having a (usually vertical) frequency axis and a (usually horizontal) intensity axis.

To compare two populations by plotting them on the same axes, we will use the same frequency range but may find a different intensity range. Thus comparing the size of two species, such as men and mice, similar curves will result but they will be widely separated on the intensity, or size, axis.

The reason that the frequency of the intensity of a polygenetic feature follows a bell-shaped curve is usually because there is as much disadvantage to the animal with too great an intensity as too little. For example, a monkey's tail provides an advantage in climbing trees, provided it is not too short. On the other hand, if it were too long, it would become an awkward, dangerous encumbrance - without, at the same time, increasing the animal's ability to climb. There is, therefore, an optimum length that will be selected and since those monkeys with this particular length of tail will survive in the greatest numbers, that length occurs most frequently and therefore approaches the average in the distribution curve of tail length (which is the intensity factor for this feature) against frequency. In fact the intensity of each polygenetic trait in a species will, as the result of the action of selective pressures, tend to approach a **functional optimum** that approximates the average for the population. This will be true for all the many polygenetic traits that characterize a species.

Thus it follows, that the most successful members of a species are those that exhibit the largest number of traits with an intensity that is at or near the functional optimum for that trait. This is a significant point to which I will refer later.

Gene Refluxing

An important process that tends to reduce variability in populations is what we might term **gene refluxing**. This process, which operates especially among animals because of their mobility, brings about the separation of specific genes in the vicinity of the boundary between **niches**. As a hypothetical example, consider a mammal living at the base of a mountain. As its population increases and it seeks new territory, some individuals will move higher up the mountain slopes. However, these individuals will encounter a colder climate and be turned back by it.

A few individuals possessing a gene, or gene complex, for a heavier fur coat will persevere so that the frequency for that gene will be higher at higher elevations. Not all offspring of individuals having this gene will inherit it, however, and those not having it will be forced to migrate back down the mountain. At the same time, some of the variants living at the lower elevation, who, although they do not have a heavy coat, carry the gene for it, will occasionally produce offspring who do, and these will join the ones at higher elevations.

Thus there will be a flow of the gene for a heavy coat up the mountain while its allele for the lighter coat moves down. This produces two new populations, which at first are only variants or races of the original species. Since they now occupy different niches, however, they will come under different selective pressures, causing them to diverge even further with the result that separate species may develop.

Gene refluxing could also cause separation in populations in which the characteristic being selected for is polygenetic. In this case there would be a gradation in the intensity of expression of the characteristic from one niche to another.

Gene Refluxing Promotes Multiple Simultaneous Changes

To complete a successful exploitation of a new region, or way of life, usually requires that a species undergoes changes in a number of its physical and behavioral traits. The likelihood that mutations resulting in such changes would occur simultaneously in a single organism is remote. However, it is possible that the mutations could occur in separate individuals and eventually be combined in a single individual as the result of mating, but this too is a slow process in a large population. Even to establish a single new trait would take a long time, particularly if the gene produced by the mutation is recessive, since to be expressed, and therefore to confer an advantage on an individual, mating would have to occur between two bearers of the same gene, an event with a low probability in a large population.

On the other hand, if the trait provides its bearer with even a slight advantage in, or affinity for, the new niche, that animal will tend to spend more time in the new niche than other animals not possessing the novel trait. In time it may be joined by others similarly endowed and since the new population will initially be small and local, the frequency of the new genes will be high, and become even higher in the new environment due to gene refluxing. Other advantageous traits will also be concentrated in the new environment, particularly if they, in combination with the first, confer a marked advantage on those individuals possessing both traits. Thus gene refluxing can increase - not only the likelihood of establishing a single change in a species - but of multiple contemporaneous changes as well.

One region in which refluxing must have been particularly active would have been in the inter-tidal zone during the period when life was migrating from the sea to the land. Any animal that could leave the water for even a brief period would have had a distinct advantage over its fellows in avoiding predators and obtaining food. Since this attribute would, no doubt, be polygenetic - involving many factors - there would have been a selection of those possessing this trait with the highest intensity.

Gene refluxing between a larger, older region and a newer, smaller one, has the advantage - not only of an increased frequency of combing traits in the smaller niche - but also of having available a larger, more generous source of mutants provided by the larger population in the older region.

Objections to the Evolutionary Theory

Objections to the theory of evolution mainly hinge on the supposed fact that it is not 'falsifiable', or is 'untestable'. However, should - for example - the bones of a mammal appear embedded in a stratum of Cambrian rock, the theory would suffer an immediate and devastating falsification. Thus it is obvious that the discovery of each new fossil constitutes another test of the theory, and since tens of thousands of such discoveries have been made without a single *authenticated* deviation from the proposed order of descent being recorded, such objections are untenable.

But What is Success?

Herbert Spencer defined natural selection as '**survival of the fittest**'. Detractors of Darwin's theories attacked this phrase as being no more than a tautology, which it is if one defines 'fitness' as 'the ability to survive'. Darwin, however, defined fitness as, not only the ability to survive, but to reproduce as well. We may conclude, therefore, that nature selects those survivors who succeed in reproducing.

An even more accurate and inclusive definition of a **successful** or **fit individual** is - *one whose offspring reproduce*. The importance of this definition is that it includes the function of providing for the survival of as many of one's offspring as possible. Thus, some examples of fit individuals would include:

- A plant that produces a large number of seeds, each containing sufficient nutrients to nourish its seedlings until they are able to provide for themselves and encloses them in a fruit that entices animals to scatter them

- The lioness that feeds and protects her cubs until they reach puberty.

- Humans who join a group, tribe or society for their own and their offspring's protection.

Judging Success

Perhaps the best criterion for judging the **success of a species** is to assess its population, which should be either stable or increasing. By this criterion, turtles are extremely successful since their population has remained essentially unchanged for over 200 million years. The species *Homo sapiens* is, at the moment, also highly successful, since its numbers continue to grow at an accelerating rate.

A **successful gene** is considered to be one that contributes to the success of its carrier and is thereby itself reproduced, resulting in an increase of its frequency in the gene pool.

There is no guarantee of continuing success for any species, however, since environmental changes can rapidly eradicate the successful status of any group of individuals and cause a reduction in its numbers. Such a population is said to be under **stress** or under pressure. If the result of this pressure is to reduce the numbers of a segment of the population relative to the remainder, the population is said to be under **selective pressure**.

CHAPTER TWO

A HYPOTHETICAL EXAMPLE

From what has been said so far, two important observations should be noted.

- All the characteristics an organism possesses are those that have survived the tests imposed by natural selection, allowing us to conclude that all organisms are products of the evolutionary processes.

- The traits, or characteristics, exhibited by mammals are instilled in them by genes that they inherit from their parents. Many traits are the products of the action of a number of genes and since inheritance is governed by the laws of chance, any such trait will be expressed in the members of a population by a range of intensities.

To illustrate how the various selective mechanisms we have been discussing could produce the evolutionary changes we have observed, let us consider the effect they would have on a hypothetical animal species. As we initially observe it, the species is under no excessive selective pressures, or is for the moment 'successful' - which is to say that its numbers are either constant or increasing. Given enough time, the physical size of all its members will correspond to that predicted by the normal distribution curve. Most individuals will be close to the average size, (which will be the functional optimum in a stable population) but a few will be somewhat larger and a few smaller (Curve 1, Figure 2).

Now suppose that a predator with which they are unfamiliar moves into their area. Initially the predator will have *carte blanche* finding our animal an easy prey, and as a consequence will increase rapidly in numbers as it depletes the prey. A few of the prey will escape extinction, however, due to their size; the smallest since they are able to scurry into undergrowth that few of the predators can penetrate and the larger since they are able to out-run the predator due to their strength and size. There will, then, be a decrease in those prey whose size is closest to the average, resulting in a drastic change in the shape of the size distribution curve.

The original such curve will be similar to that for the height-of-men curve (Figure 1A), but will rapidly change from this form (curve 1, Figure 2) to the bimodal curve (2A and B) shown in Figure 2. Although bimodal, this distribution does not have the same origin as that in Figure 1B, since each peak, although much narrower than the original, will itself show an approximately normal distribution. From this it is evident that two populations have now replaced the first. Furthermore, the members of each of the new populations will occupy different geographical regions or niches - the larger in open grassland and the smaller in bush land - and will no longer interbreed.

These are ideal curves which would, in reality, be fused into one another over time, resulting in a slow drift of the new peaks along the intensity (size) axis as the initial population divides into two.

Due to the small number of individuals comprising each of these two new populations, the variance in characteristics of both will be correspondingly less than they were in the initial single population, even when their numbers recover from the initial attack. This is known as the **founders effect**, which refers to the much *decreased genetic pool available to a newly established population and results from the fact that all subsequent members are descendants of a comparatively few individuals*. Thus there will be a reduction in the variability, not only of the relative sizes of the individuals but also of all their other traits - physical, behavioral, biochemical and immunological.

This depletion in variability occurs, not only because individuals have been selected *per se*, but because the number of individuals in each population has been reduced as well. As a result, both new populations will be extremely vulnerable at first, since they will no longer have the genetic

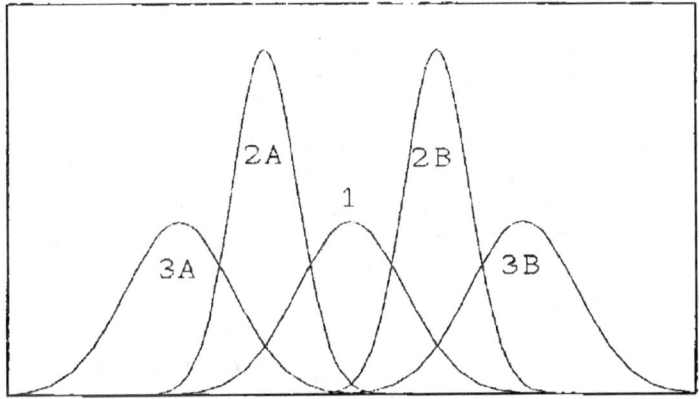

Figure 2: Fate of the hypothetical animal population following an attack by a predator. The curves are plots of size (horizontal axis) against the percentage of individuals having that size (vertical axis).

Curve 1 – Before the attack.
Curves 2A and 2B – immediately after the attack.
Curves 3A and 3B – The same following a period during which mutations have increased variability in the two population

reserves that the population from which they were derived had, to absorb a sudden further attack. For example, the appearance of a disease to which even one individual in either population proves susceptible, could be disastrous, since others (in the same population) would probably succumb as well, due to the genetic similarity of their immune systems.

But the Predator is Also Altered by Selection

The predator, following its initial invasion and decimation of the prey, will find itself subject to the stress of a reduced food supply, and will, as a result, also be altered by selection. At first, the faster and larger predators will be successful in capturing the larger prey so that the gene line specifying the larger predators will increase in frequency. At the same time, members of the smaller predator population will also be successful since they will be able to pursue the smaller prey into its proposed sanctuary.

Mutation as a Dispersive Force

Should the prey in our example flourish and grow in numbers, there will be a gradual increase in variability, and a broadening of the distribution curves (curves 3A and 3B, Fig. 2) of each of the traits possessed by their descendants due to **mutations** in their genetic material. This process, which occurs naturally in all living things, results from *alterations to the chemical structure of the usually highly stable genetic material as a result of natural radiation, the action of teratogenic compounds, or simply because all chemical reactions, such as the synthesis of new genetic material, are basically random in nature and do not invariably follow the same course.*

Such changes, which occur with a fairly predictable frequency, are random and may affect any of the organisms' functions. In the vast majority of cases they result in changes that are detrimental, or more usually, fatal to the individual - as when the gene for an essential enzyme or hormone is destroyed - and are therefore not propagated. Many are neutral or mild in their effects causing only slight changes in various proteins and the functions they perform in the individual. A few are beneficial, however, and provide their possessors with some advantage towards surviving and reproducing, and, as a result, the genes specifying this new attribute increase in frequency within the local population. Such changes require many, perhaps thousands of generations to occur, but taken over a long time period, the accumulative effect of all these changes is to increase profoundly the variability of many of the animal's characteristic features.

The Action of Conservative Forces

This broadening effect does not go on indefinitely, however, since opposing **conservative forces** are also operating. One of these forces is the usual 'natural selection'. Again taking size as our example trait, the larger specimens of the small animal population may once more fall prey to predators, while the smaller individuals fail to win mates. At the same time, an inability of the largest animals to obtain sufficient food will limit the upper size in the population of the larger animals while the predator will continue to limit their lower size.

In addition, however, there is another conservative force that the species itself imposes on the individual - one that we have already considered - restrictive mating. In the initial population, the most successful, and therefore the most numerous animals will have been those nearest the average in size since the population was not originally under pressure and was, therefore, in a steady state. The pressure imposed by the predator, however, will have drastically reduced the numbers of the original sexual clique since they will have ceased to be the most successful (or are, under the new conditions, maladapted) and the offspring of any individuals continuing to mate with them will be at risk.

However, the gene-imposed desire to choose a mate of a specific size is also itself a polygenetic trait. This means that although the majority of survivors will continue to seek a mate from the remaining members of the original sexual clique, there will be some individuals among the smaller animals whose desires are for mates smaller than the average of the initial population. It will be from their offspring that the more 'successful' individuals in the new population will derive. Thus with time, a new standard of sexual preference will be established by selection in the smaller animals. A similar shift towards a preference for larger mates will also occur amongst the larger animals.

The overall effect on the original prey population caused by the attack of the predators will be that their frequency-size distribution curve will be split into two new curves, one of which will be pushed by the pressure due to predation along the size axis toward lower values, while the other will shift in the opposite direction. Or put another way, the size of each population will approach its new functional optimum.

The sexual size-preference-versus-frequency curve will follow a similar but slower course. It will therefore be some time before the average of this curve corresponds to that of the average size-distribution-versus-frequency curve of the two new populations. Initially these distribution curves will be broad and indistinct, since there will be a number of possible combinations of traits, some of which may have higher survival possibilities than others. With time, the population of the most efficacious mixes will increase at the expense of the others, and it will be on the members of these groups that sexual preference will eventually focus. This focusing will be promoted by the offspring of those whose preference is to mate with the more successful individuals, since they themselves will tend to be successful and will carry genes for this preference. The resulting positive feedback will increase the peak of each of the distribution curves, and at the same time narrow them, leading to a more well defined species.

The Species is Defined by a Balance of Forces.

As we have noted, mutations occur in all species at a fairly constant rate and act as a **dispersive force** by *bringing about an increase in the variety of offspring produced, or a broadening of the size-distribution curve*. On the other hand, we have also seen that **natural selection** and **restrictive mating** are **conservative** or **restrictive forces** since they act in such a way as to *reduce variations in a species and to narrow the distribution peaks*. From the conflict between these opposing forces there is selected a new functional optimum, or steady state balance, and it is *this balance that ultimately defines the species*.

But this balance is only reached provided the species is not subjected to further severe pressures. It is seldom, however, that a species is not under at least mild selective pressures. The usual situation in a highly competitive environment is that a species is constantly under assault from many directions and a slight shift in the intensity of any one of these will cause a drift away from equilibrium.

Some of these stresses are long-lasting, as for example those produced by a slowly changing climate, and result in a gradual shift in the genetic pool of the species as it is altered by changes in selective pressures. As an example, a cooling climate may result in the selection of those individuals possessing a heavier coat of fur.

A change may also arise in a species which is not under pressure due to the occurrence of an advantageous mutation. Detrimental mutations, which occur far more frequently, will have little effect, however, since they will rapidly be eliminated by selection.

Behavioral Strategies May Also Evolve

Physiological changes are not the only means by which those animals pursuing the larger prey can increase their success, however, and we can expect accompanying behavioral changes to occur as well. These could take the form of changes in hunting strategy. For example, the larger predators might overcome the increased speed of the prey by employing greater stealth in approaching their victims before launching their final assault, or they might combine efforts with others of their kind in a communal attack. Again individuals utilizing these hunting strategies will be more successful in promoting their own welfare and those of their offspring, and so will perpetuate the gene complex specifying these behaviors.

As with the predator, not all advantageous changes in the prey will be physical - many will be behavioral as well. Thus, the prey may congregate in herds for their joint protection. Any family living outside the herd would be particularly vulnerable since if one or both parents were killed, the young would have little hope of survival, while in a herd the death of its parents still leaves the young with the protection of the remaining animals.

Behavioral Changes Frequently Accompany Physical Changes

Turning now to the smaller members of our original population, these animals may pursue a different route to avoid predation. They may, for example, adopt the technique of burrowing to provide themselves with a haven. Again this will probably not be a rational or planned activity. Instead, the act of digging will likely start with some animals having an inherent desire to dig for no purpose or reason that they are aware of. Since digging will expose grubs or roots, which are useful as food, those individuals that partake of this activity will have an advantage, particularly in times of food shortage, and will consequently become more numerous. In time this trait will show the usual variance, with some individuals being more enthusiastic in their digging than the average and others less so. The more enthusiastic exponents will tend to dig deeper, providing themselves with burrows into which they can retire in response to an attack by predators, and at the same time, providing a sanctuary for their offspring. Amongst these there will be a few who also possess the physiological advantage of larger and stronger front limbs and claws. Such characteristics will likely be polygenetic and in combination with the desire to dig will provide such individuals with even safer havens and an even greater chance of survival.

Again I would stress that the animal must possess not only the physical ability to dig its burrow, but the urge to do so as well. Either trait by itself would give some advantage, but those individuals possessing both would have the greatest survival rate. The burrowing must precede the need, since most attacks by predators will be sudden and provide little time for a last minute escape. This means that the animal requires either an intellectual foresight sufficient to allow it to plan its haven in advance of an anticipated attack - or simply a mindless urge to dig a deep hole. I suggest that since the latter is less complex, it is more easily programmed into the animal and statistically should prove to be the more reliable.

Other Strategies

The sudden changes that our two fictional prey populations have undergone will provide them with only a temporary respite from the ravaging predator. Slowly then, the pressure is once more applied to the prey, in whom selection of individuals according to their size will again prevail. Eventually, however, a limit will be reached beyond which size change is no longer practical since it starts to impose other penalties that outweigh those of predation. For example, in the case of the larger animal, as its mass increases, the ability of its skeletal structure to support it may be limited, resulting in frequent accidents among the larger individuals; or it may not be able to satisfy its increased need for food; or it may prove to be a more attractive target for the predator. There may be many other reasons for an upper size limit that are fatal either individually or in combination. We see, then, that the mechanism of natural selection does not necessarily maximize or minimize the intensity of any feature, but rather, it **optimizes** it.

At the same time, there will, no doubt, be other characteristics of the prey that may be altered by selection to increase its survival rate. One such characteristic is the animal's coloring, since the more visibly obvious individuals will attract the predator's attention first, while those who blend in with their surroundings escape.

Multiple Branching and Extinction Are Also Possible

The above hypothetical animal example has provided one possible explanation for the formation of a bifurcation in the animal family tree. Such events have been quite common during evolution, not only in the case of the descent of animals, but of all organisms and in each case has resulted in the production of two divergent species, both of which are descendants of the same ancestral species. Each of the two new populations in our example was beset by different pressures and would have evolved along different paths. Since each occupied a separate niche, interbreeding between the two populations would cease and in time the two would become separate species.

We could generalize even further by noting that there may be changes to several characteristics of a species that provide relief from the pressure. Individuals possessing these features to a high degree will also be selected, an eventuality that would result in the production of a multitude of branches stemming from the initial species. This will be especially so for species under pressure.

It should also be noted that selective pressures do not always split a population as our example above has posited. In fact it is more likely throughout evolutionary history that selective pressures have eliminated those individuals who possess a particular trait to either a greater of less degree than the average. Thus in our previous example it could have been that either the larger or the smaller individuals were completely eliminated from the population, depending on the nature of the applied pressure, or in this case, on the size of the predator relative to the prey. Furthermore, our example illustrated the effect of the application of a sudden intense stress to the population, which was so close to being critical, that, had it been only slightly more intense, or combined with another threat, would have resulted in complete annihilation of the species, a common event throughout the history of evolution. Even for less intense pressures, which result in a correspondingly more gradual change to the species under stress, the mechanism will be the same - the elimination of one part of the spectrum of traits that the species exhibits - or in statistical terms - a shift in the frequency peak along the intensity axis. More time for mutations will be afforded, however, allowing the species to maintain its variability during this selection period.

The Plasticity of Characteristics

All characteristics of living populations are dynamic in nature and readily yield to pressure. Thus a frequency-distribution peak that is depressed at one intensity, may reappear at another. In the example above we considered a change in only one characteristic - the size of the animal. Any characteristic that gives some animals an advantage will also be shifted along its frequency axis and in fact probably many such shifts will come into play. Some of these will have been present in a small number of mutant individuals, and while appearing eccentric and therefore suppressed by mate selection during stasis, may prove to enhance their survival - and therefore increase their frequency - under pressure. Thus, the species will show a shift in many directions in response to changes in its environment. One might think of the topography of these peaks as being plastic in nature, so that when pushed in at one point, simply rise up at one or more points in different directions and distances away from the first. Realizing this, one is tempted to question the reality of the claim that so many species have become 'extinct' rather than merely 'modified'.

The 'plasticity' in the characteristics of a species derives from its genetic variability, which represents an important reserve that all species must have to survive the inevitable pressures they experience.

Selective Pressure Can Result in an Outburst of Speciation.

While a species is in a steady state, or **stasis**, there is little tolerance for mutants, which are usually eliminated by conservative forces. This produces a feedback effect, which tends to prolong stasis. With the imposition of an acute selective pressure, however, mate selection is disrupted and, since it takes longer to re-establish than the new functional optimum, there will be a period of increased tolerance toward mutants. Thus a number of variants will appear, many of which may prove to be successful in different ways. We see, then, that following the imposition of a selective pressure of sufficient intensity to overcome the conservative forces, a burst of **speciation** may result.

A species under pressure, or **stress** - which we now see can be defined as *a shift in environmental conditions such that many of the traits that previously contributed to the success of the individual, no longer do so* - can, and usually does, result in simultaneous shifts in many traits. Thus, as a corollary, when we observe a species that appears to be undergoing speciation, i.e., showing a large number of variations, we may conclude that, *that species is under pressure.*

A successful species seldom undergoes change, and therefore, natural selection produces its greatest changes in a species when it is subjected to stress. Thus we may conclude that *evolution is a product of stress.*

Speciation May Be Random as well as Stress-Induced

A species need not be under stress to speciate, however. A new population may arise from one that is well established and stable through gene refluxing into an adjacent niche. We have already mentioned that such a mechanism must have been active during the initial invasion of land by marine organisms. In such a case the initial species need not become extinct but may continue to thrive unchanged far into the future in parallel with its derivative on land.

Evolutionary Jumps - Apparent or Real?

We have dealt here with mechanisms for change in populations of animals, which, although they may be rapid or slow, are, nevertheless, continuous. Some of the more rapid changes may appear to be instantaneous according to the record of the fossil remains available to us, simply because they occurred so rapidly that the remains of the intermediate forms were not preserved - or were so few in number that we have not yet discovered them. This, no doubt, explains the majority of apparently sudden changes we observe.

Nevertheless, we should not preclude the possibility that there have been incidences in which a sudden drastic change in the genes of one individual due to mutation was introduced into the gene pool of a species. The more drastic the change in a trait, however, the greater the number of other features that may have to be altered simultaneously to compensate for what might otherwise be a fatal distortion of the mutant's bodily functions, and the greater the number of simultaneous changes required, the less frequently can such changes have taken place. Still, given the enormous number of changes that living things have undergone throughout history, such events must have been responsible for some of the major shifts in the direction that evolution has taken.

The fossil record also teaches us that there have been times during geological history when violent and far-reaching events have occurred, bringing enormous pressures to bear on virtually all existing species. These pressures appear to have destroyed many species that did not have the genetic reserves from which to draw in order to survive.

The Importance of Genetic Reserves

Finally we should again stress the importance of genetic variability to a species. As we have seen, such diversity promotes the possibility that there will be individuals in the population whose form or behavior allows them to flourish following alterations in the environment. The greater the diversity of individuals within a population, the greater the probability that a variant able to resist any given pressure is present to continue the gene line.

Subsequent to the imposition of pressure, the species exhibits a change in the frequency of variants within its population. This is commonly referred to as: "an adaptation of the species to a change in its surroundings.", an unfortunate declaration implying that the species itself somehow takes an active part in this process. Any modification in the species that occurs, however, results from the operation of the selective process, in which the species has no part to play. Thus we should define **adaptation** of a species as *the selection of variants capable of surviving an applied pressure.*

The amount of variability a species exhibits should be an important factor for us to consider when examining the effect the drastic reduction in population we are currently inflicting on a number of species, has on those species. Although we may have - for the moment - rescued many from the brink of extinction, we may, at the same time, have robbed them of the wealth of diversity that required tens or even hundreds of thousands of years for them to accumulate. In doing so, we may have imposed a debilitating **founders effect** on them - condemning them to a doubtful future!

CHAPTER THREE

EMOTION AND REASON

"Le Coeur a des raisons que la raisin ne connait pas."[1] - Pascal

As animals evolved into more complex organisms, natural selection favored those individuals possessing *inherent* emotions that functioned in such a manner as to compel or urge them to respond or act in ways proven by previous success to be in their own best interests. Most of these emotional drives - usually termed 'instincts' in the less complex animals - had to be present in the animal right from the moment it began its separate existence, since it had neither the ability nor the time to learn the behaviors that promoted its welfare, or even its survival. This was especially so, since a single mistake could be fatal.

Among the more important drives, or emotions, are hunger - which promotes almost constant foraging for food, and, when threatened, either fear - which leads to flight or withdrawal, or anger - which leads to fighting.

---

[1] "The heart has reasons of which reason knows naught."

But while these drives may be sufficient for the immediate survival of the individual, they alone are not enough to perpetuate its gene complement. In addition, the individual must also possess genes for traits that promote reproduction, such as a sex drive leading to mating, and a desire to protect and provide for its offspring.

All these drives, or emotions, are unquestionably inherited since the activity they promote need not be learned and are absolutely essential for the survival, welfare of the individual, and perpetuation of the genes carried by the individual. In short, the successful gene complement is one that specifies that the individual carrying it behaves in ways that optimize its own chances for success.

The Function of Intelligence

It is not enough for an animal to possess urges to act in its own best interests, however, since it must also have the ability to pursue these urges. The genes provide this ability, by furnishing the animal with the power of movement and the ability to sense its surroundings, as well as a memory and the intelligence to make beneficial decisions when necessary. Thus, animal **behavior** is determined by two forces - *the emotions and the intellect*. I would like to suggest, therefore, that we consider our minds as being essentially **bicameral**, since they appear to be composed of two functionally separate parts - one of which can be specified as the **primitive** or emotional mind, the other as the **rational** or decision-making mind.

As we have previously noted, we use the term **emotion** when referring to the stronger feelings, such as fear, anger, hate, jealousy, love, etc., with which we humans are familiar. And like other animals, our response to these feelings is moderated by our intelligence. Thus, even while possessed by a fear that amounts to panic, we are still able to direct our steps toward the exit of a burning building. Furthermore, the intellect is necessary to provide the initial reason for the arousal of the emotion since we must first interpret the sight of flames, the smell of smoke or the meaning of the shout: "FIRE!" before we can experience the emotion. Nevertheless, the overwhelming urge that provides the immediate goal - *to escape the danger at all costs* - is provided by the emotions, not by the intellect. It is the intellect's function to determine the means by which that goal is to be achieved.

I would like to redefine the term **emotions** as **inherent urges that constitute the sole and ultimate initiators of all actions taken by animals.**

This definition implies that emotional directives, or urges, function by compelling the animal to act in ways that promote its welfare and, in so doing, increasing the probability that the genes specifying these emotional responses will be selected and thereby propagated. Thus the emotions and the genes themselves, form a positive feedback loop that guarantees the retention of both in the individual, with the genes instilling the drives and the drives promoting the propagation of these genes.

In humans this definition would include all the motivations, cravings, longings, yearnings, urges, likes, dislikes, fancies, desires, hungers, obsessions, passions, preferences, partialities, predilections, propensities, crazes, fetishes, phobias, fixations, manias, etc., which are inherent in our make-up.

Goals, on the other hand, **are rational constructs that direct our behavior towards alleviating the pressure imposed by emotions**. Thus in response to the emotion 'hunger' one might set the goal 'to catch a fish' since our reason tells us that by doing so one might dispel the pressure imposed by the emotion. The same goal might also be fashioned simply because, to reach such a goal (to catch a fish) would give one pleasure.

It is not necessarily essential to the success of a gene that we attain our goals. What is important is that in striving to do so, we take actions that procure our success.

All Our Ultimate Goals Are Set by Our Emotions - None by Our Intellect.

These definitions, however, have what might seem to be an outrageous corollary - which is that *all our ultimate goals are initiated in response to pressures imposed by our emotions - none arise directly from our intellect!* There is, for example, no intellectual justification for continuing to live, only our inherent *desire* to do so - our *will* to live and our *fear* of dying, which I classify as **emotional imperatives**. No gene complement that did not imbue its carrier with the primary goal of prolonging its own life would be likely to be propagated and would soon become extinct. Organisms capable of conscious thought perceive this goal as a powerful, almost irresistible *urge*. Through our emotions the genes direct our behavior along lines that promote our welfare and their propagation. We consider ourselves to be essentially rational beings, but in fact our emotions influence our rational processes profoundly - at times overwhelming them. If we exhaustively question any of our goals, ultimately they are reduced to statements containing such words as *want, wish, desire*, etc., all of which are charged with emotional content.

Instinct and emotion formed the basis of the primitive mind, while intellect and reasoning are more recently evolved additions. Our intellect, like our physical attributes, is servant to our emotions, constantly searching for ways with which to gratify its master; providing memory, planning the means by which we may attain such needs as food and sexual partners and, at times, adjudicating between conflicting emotions (such as whether to fight or flee). Like an automobile, our intelligence is but a machine that performs acts directed by its operator - our emotions. Or like a computer, our rationality has no goals other than those supplied by the programmer - our genes, which furnish the code in the form of emotional directives. In short, our emotions provide the mind's agenda. We have the illusion of rational control since on frequent occasions our intellect must provide immediate decisions as to the next action we should take. But powerful as it is, it is seldom a match for our most intense emotions - our passions. It is through the emotions that the genes are able to specify that the actions the individual takes are those most likely to be in its own best interests. No gene complement that did not provide such guidance would be likely to be propagated.

The behavior and many of the beliefs we exhibit today are those that are specified by genes that have weathered the judgement of natural selection during a lengthy past.

But the actions of the individual cannot be too limited by the emotions since there must be some flexibility to deal with the variety of challenges an animal is likely to face during its lifetime. It is to moderate the rigidity of a purely instinctive response that the intellect is called upon. Obviously, for each species, there is an optimum balance between the relative level of control the emotions and the intellect exercise over the actions of the individual, and this balance is usually attained, at least approximately, by natural selection.

Thus it will be a recurring theme in this work - that *the ultimate goals of every animal are specified by its genetic complement, not its intelligence, which functions instead in assisting the animal to attain these goals.* A bird can have no knowledge of why it builds its nest - only a *desire* to do so, and the inherent knowledge of how to go about the construction - which we call instinct. In fact there is no advantage whatsoever to the bird in questioning the purpose of the nest, even if it had the mental capacity to do so. The one essential requirement is that the nest be ready in time to receive the eggs. Since many of the young cannot have seen their parents building their nest, they can have no memory of this process, nor even any concept of its ultimate use when they set about building one themselves. This is especially so since the birds building the nest are unaware of the fact that they are about to produce their own offspring. While their inherent instinct provides the goal and the drive, it is their intellect that directs them in selecting a site, obtaining the materials required for construction and transporting them to the site - *but not in furnishing a reason for this activity.*

To generalize, then, we may conclude that *emotions command - reason counsels!* **There is no intellectual imperative!** Furthermore, we may define **behavior** as *the actions we take in our attempts to attain the goals we seek* - goals that have been instilled in us by genes whose persistence in the gene line derives from the contribution their products have made to the success of our species.

How Would a Totally Rational, Unemotional Human Act?
Consider such a person in a burning building. An emotional person would - as we have already noted - immediately attempt to escape. The unemotional person, however, even though he would have a complete appraisal of his situation as provided by his senses, as well as the *ability* to escape, would make no move to do so, since he would have no feelings of *fear* or *concern* for his safety. As he possessed no *curiosity,* he would not even turn his attention to the approaching flames.

But would he not feel pain?

Pain consists of two components - **sensation - nervous impulses reporting damage to the body** and **perception - a genetically instilled emotional imperative to regard the sensation with intense 'dislike'**. The perception would, of course, be lacking in our subject and would therefore not motivate him to escape. His body would twitch and writhe since his reflexes would still function. Observing him, we would think him mad, even though he was in fact highly rational, since it would be inconceivable to us that a rational person, even one not feeling pain, would not attempt to save himself in such a situation! The fact is, however, that *without emotion there can be no premise upon which a logical conclusion to initiate any physical movement whatsoever can be based!* Once again we see that, while the intellect may *moderate* actions taken by the body, it is incapable of *initiating* them!

Can Computers Become Human?

There is a common misconception, amongst many science fiction (and even some semi-serious) writers, that increasing the intelligence of a computer will inevitably make it human, or even superhuman. This arises from the egotistical supposition that humans are essentially rational beings whose most important characteristic is their intelligence. In fact, it is not their intelligence that makes people human, but rather, their inherent emotions. Intelligence is certainly an important human characteristic in much the same way as walking upright is, but it does not guide our behavior to anything like the same extent as that of our emotions.

Thus, increasing the speed and ability with which a computer is able to resolve complex Boolean relationships, and providing it with an ever increasing memory bank, will not cause it to perform even such an essentially human act as resisting its own destruction - unless specifically programmed to do so! Thus, if we want a humanoid computer, we must provide it with the same goals most humans possess at birth.

Are There No Purely Intellectually driven Acts?

"But just a minute!" you might say, as you pick up a pencil here and put it down there, "Was that not an act completely devoid of any emotional content?"

Was it? Would you have performed such an act if you did not *want* to? And why would you want to? Would it not be in response to the urging of your ego whose sole function is to compel you to advance yourself personally, to win a point and to prove that we, as a humans, are members of a species that is superior to all others in its ability to divest itself of the vulgar bonds of emotion - and to float freely in the pure clear air of the intellect?

When asked to provide the ultimate reasons for the goals we adopt, our explanations are invariably reduced to statements containing words of emotional content, such as *want* or its equivalent. Thus we might be asked a simple question such as: "Why do you go to university?" To this question we are tempted to reply: "Because I want to learn.", but realizing that this implies emotional bias, we reply instead: "Because I need to learn."   In response to the obvious query as to why we 'need' this knowledge, our reply takes such form as: "Because I have to make money." And for what purpose? "To support myself and my family." Such goals can hardly be construed as unemotional!

Emotions May Be Positive or Negative

Emotions may be classified as positive or negative (phobic or philic), depending on the response that they induce in the individual. Just as primitive animals move away from physical conditions that are either too hot or too cold and towards food and sexual partners, our emotions urge us either to avoid or to seek certain objects or situations depending on whether we associate those objects or situations with feelings of *pain* or *pleasure*. **Pain** is a very powerful deterrent for a very good reason - it is associated with damage to our bodies. Through it we are taught to avoid actions that are, or could be, injurious. If we did not feel an intense desire to avoid pain, we would not survive to propagate, which is why *pain is inherently painful!*

For the same reason, those things that promote our welfare and cause us to reproduce are associated with **pleasure**. Thus there appear to be two diametrically opposed centers in our brains - one evoking pleasure and the other pain or displeasure, and each of our emotions is associated - or connected - with one, and only one, of these centers.

Summary

The mind is essentially bimodal and operates at two levels - the emotional and the rational. The emotional mind provides the individual with goals and urges that direct its behavior. These goals and urges are instilled in the individual by genes whose propagation depends on the behavior they induce in their carriers. Behavior promoting the welfare of the individual and its ability to survive, to reproduce and to assist its own offspring in reaching maturity will ensure the propagation of those genes inducing such behavior.

The rational mind provides the individual with the ability to engage in unemotional reasoning. Like any rational system, however, human reasoning is a sequential process and therefore must stem from premises provided by an external source. In sentient animals, this source is the genetically induced goals resident in the emotional mind. So it is that *emotions provide the premises for existence.*

In undertaking the reasoning process, the rational mind first assembles all the available data. This includes information provided by the senses, the memory and the nerves reporting on the present position and direction of movement of all parts of the body. With the immediate intention of the emotional mind as its premise, this data is subjected to a rational analysis and a decision is reached as to the next action to be taken by the body. The appropriate muscular stimuli are then issued by the rational mind.

The rational mind is also constantly engaged in assessing the progress being made toward attaining the goals desired by the individual, and in informing the emotional mind of the successes or failures in this regard. The emotional mind then responds to this assessment by injecting **feelings** into the stream of consciousness - feelings of pleasure as a reward for success, and sadness, frustration, anger or fear as punishment when the goals are in jeopardy.

Feelings are the *means by which our emotions communicate with our conscious mind.* They add weight to the goals directing the decisions an individual is attempting to make, such as when fear is given a greater weight than hunger by the emotional mind in response to an assessment provided by the rational mind, and thus becomes the premise upon which immediate decisions are to be made.

Consciousness is probably a product of the emotional mind, since it is rife with feelings, which are, in reality, simply emotional responses to the assessments provided by the rational mind.

Examples

The following are some examples of emotional drives that affect our behavior, but usually escape definition as 'emotions':

Egoism

Egoism is *the tendency to be self-centered, to consider only one's self and one's own interests*. It is not usually termed an emotion, but under the present definition it becomes so, since it is an important inherent urge affecting our behavior. It is usually considered to be contemptible since it tends to oppose the demands of the society in which we live, but none could survive without it. Our immediate needs must be met if we are to endure and flourish. It is for this reason that egoism is one of the most powerful *and persistent* emotions we harbor.

Altruism

Altruism - *the unselfish concern for the welfare of others* - is the antithesis of egoism. It is essential to our welfare, since it assists us in joining with others to form the societies that sustain us and our offspring. Such an emotion must be genuine to be effective and furthermore must not be too powerful, since, if so, it can be detrimental to the individual. A proper balance between egoism and altruism is vital, and such a balance, or functional optimum, has been instilled in the average human by selective forces. The importance of this trait will be discussed further below.

Curiosity

The survival value of most of our emotions is quite obvious, but why we are driven by curiosity is perhaps less obvious. Curiosity appears to be an emotion shared by most animals. *It is an urge, rather than a rational direction, to obtain information, whether this information is of immediate use to the animal or not*. Obviously it requires the intellect to perceive, assess, and store the information, but the driving force is the pleasure that the individual experiences in pursuing the goal. This pleasure is evident to anyone who has ever taken a dog for a walk in the countryside and seen him, with every sense alert, ranging through grass, brush, and wood. Even though he has just been fed and is not, therefore, being driven by hunger, the pleasure he feels in performing this natural function is evident in the eagerness and energy he displays. So too with humans, for whom, particularly in their primitive state, information was vital. While being pursued by a predator is not the time to be familiarizing oneself with the topography and the location of possible havens!

The design and use of tools must have originated with the rise in the intellectual abilities of early man. However, it would not have been enough for him to depend on his intellect alone to suggest the shape of the tools he required. A much more fruitful approach would have arisen from a *desire* to undertake a haphazard examination of the objects and materials at his disposal, testing various methods of altering them, even without a clear idea of what might prove to be useful. Thus an extension of this natural curiosity to include the utilitarian possibilities of the various objects and materials he would have encountered must have arisen, originally by chance, and would have been retained due to its survival value, culminating in what we term 'inventiveness'. Today, these desires drive the activities we know as science and technology, which are highly regarded, providing social status and wealth to those engaged in them - rewards that add further incentive to their pursuit.

Aesthetics

The aesthetic experiences most of us have, derive, I believe, from the complexity of the human brain. We are almost totally unaware of the enormous intricacies of interwoven, and mainly forgotten, associations that have formed our minds. The purpose of the artist is to determine the visual or auditory cues that evoke pleasurable, or even disturbing, associations. Since the network of associations each of us has is the result of our own personal experience, appreciation of the arts is almost totally subjective.

Nevertheless, there are many common experiences and impressions we all share and it is through these that the artist elicits the response she or he seeks.

Because of the subjective nature of aesthetic experiences, I can only employ an incident from my own life to illustrate this point. One of the most powerful of such events occurred for me during my first encounter with the most famous of all paintings, Leonardo da Vinci's Mona Lisa, housed in the Louvre. As I suspect is true of most people, I had previously seen many copies of this well-known work, which I found had virtually no effect on me. In fact, I regarded it as a somewhat feckless painting of a half-smiling woman of no great physical beauty.

As I pondered the original, however, it suddenly underwent an apparent transformation. The sea-green background seemed to recede from the seated figure - to glow, and to be steeped in a deep and profound mystery. The insipid smile now became wise and comforting. She knew all - and her knowledge was of great beneficence.

How could a few flecks of age-darkened and cracked pigments displayed on a flat wooden surface inspire such intense feelings? Obviously the artistry of the great master enabled him to reach into the cavernous depths of the mind to pluck the strings of memory and to summon forth chords of emotions long forgotten. What could these memories be?

Considering this question, it occurred to me that the smile of La Gioconda is the smile of the Madonna - the smile of essential motherhood. The figure in the painting looks directly into the eyes of the observer, as she would those of her own child, with a comforting, reassuring smile. Through this imagery, da Vinci reminds us of the pleasures associated with a deeply emotional event common to us all, the instant when the satiated child, momentarily freed from the stresses of its new life, recognizes the mother as a person, a being who is the source of warmth and contentment, of security and nourishment. Returning her smile consummates one of the most profoundly emotional events in life - *the bonding of mother and child!*

Many would be indignant at the presumption of so simple an answer, preferring instead the unexplained mystery. For such persons, the soft edges of aesthetic beauty are hardened in the harsh glare of analysis!

Free Will

Finally, we must ask ourselves: "What choices do we *really* have? Is there no free will?" The answer (which summarizes one of the main themes of this book) is:

We cannot choose the goals we seek -
only the means by which we seek to attain them!

CHAPTER FOUR

BEHAVIORAL TRAITS

The importance of genes specified behavioral traits is that they provide a means of selecting beneficial behavior in the individual carrying them (the carrier).

Behavioral traits can be just as vital to an animal as its physical equivalents. Whether an animal is nocturnal or diurnal, for example, can affect its safety and ability to obtain food. **'Goodness'** is another such trait, which is usually ascribed only to humans, and is therefore highly subjective. I submit, however, that if we were able to quantify and plot its intensity, we would obtain an approximation to a bell-shaped curve. I say this since there are many factors that contribute to this quality and few people are either all 'good' or all 'bad'. The important thing, however, is not whether goodness is a subjective trait, but whether it contributes to an individual's success. I intend later to argue that it does, and that while a certain amount of goodness is essential for survival of the individual - too much goodness can be detrimental - which is why few of us are perfect!

In this chapter we will consider a number of behavioral traits and attempt to illustrate how they affect our welfare.

Herding

Herding is another example of the emotions providing a goal. One might argue that herding is a learned or reasoned behavior and not necessarily a genetic trait. However, I maintain that learning and reasoning are not sufficiently reliable when the safety of the individual, and particularly its offspring, are at stake. A much more consistently effective and reliable drive toward **herding** would be *an inherent emotional compulsion, which the individual experiences as a positive feeling, such as comfort and security when in the midst of the herd, and a negative feeling, such as unease or even fear when others of its species are not in sight.*

This will be particularly important when it becomes necessary for the herd to spread out to obtain food. It is at such times that the vigilance of the individual and contact with its fellows will be more effectively maintained by a constant unconscious emotional drive than by a voluntary or conscious effort, especially since the latter may suffer competition from other mental activities, such as feeding, and may therefore - in the absence of any immediate apparent danger - become lax. Without this drive, some animals might stray from the herd beyond the point from which they could safely return in the event of a sudden attack by predators.

Alarm signals.

Another behavioral trait frequently found in herding animals and flocks of birds is the issuing of an **alarm signal with which an individual notifies the other members of the herd, or flock, of impending danger.** These may be auditory, as with the alarm call of a bird - or visual, as with the flagging tail of the deer. Since such displays will call the attention of the predator to the signaling animal and increase the likelihood that any animal displaying this trait will become the victim, one may wonder how such behavior could have been selected. Natural selection does not function solely to prolong the life of the individual, however, but rather with the propagation of its gene line. Thus if the individual has already reproduced - and the chances are in favor of it having several descendants in the herd - it is more important that these offspring survive to puberty than that the older animal abandons the young and takes a chance of reproducing further. It is therefore of more value to the gene line, in most cases, for the parent to offer itself as prey in place of its offspring in a situation where its offspring have a reasonable chance to survive and to reproduce as members of a herd. Individuals exhibiting this behavior are likely to have more descendants than those that do not.

There also appears to be an urge for individuals of a herd or flock to follow the signaling member in its flight while at the same time issuing their own warnings. This guarantees that the flock or herd remains together for its own, and each individual's safety. Any animal taking flight without signaling, may end up on its own and be denied the sanctity of the group. One might even go further and suggest that the group actively excludes non-cooperative individuals by closing ranks against them - or driving them away - which will, of course, lead to the extinction of the non-cooperative members while increasing the survival of the signal-specifying genes. I am not aware of any evidence for this activity in most gregarious animals. However, there is one exception - which I propose to discuss presently - in which there is evidence that those individuals who do not cooperate are driven from the group. This exception is, of course, the human species.

Selective Mating

Few behavioral traits are as important as those related to mating, since, for a gene complement to be successful in perpetuating itself, it must influence the individual who carries it to seek out the most suitable mate from among the population and to shun unsuitable partners.

As a result, there appears to be a reluctance amongst the members of many species to mate with other individuals who differ in some way from the species norm. Thus it has been found that when two very closely related populations of the fruit fly *Drosophila* native to different geographic areas, are mixed, they mate mainly with other members of their own populations in spite of there being no discernible difference (to the human eye, at least) in the physical appearance of the two populations. Recognition of their own fellow members is probably aided by the presence of pheromones (chemical messengers) that serve to direct their mating activities in the absence of visual signals.

Many other animals, however, do employ visual means to distinguish themselves from other species, as is the case with birds whose various colorations and markings appear to serve as an aid to the individual in choosing a mate of the same species as itself.

Our observation of nature has taught us that she is highly conservative and that few of her creatures possess appendages or encumbrances that do not contribute in some way to their welfare. The reason for this seems obvious, since to maintain any useless feature requires resources supplied at the expense of the rest of the organism and in the highly competitive world in which the organism is trying to survive, any inefficiency can be fatal. Why then do most species expend considerable effort to maintain their uniformity and to decrease their variability, especially since, as we will see, a more varied genetic base provides a greater buffer in times of selective stress? There obviously must be some selective advantage to the individual in doing so, or some disadvantage in failing to do so.

Perhaps the disadvantage to an individual arises from the danger of mating with other organisms that are too dissimilar to itself. For example, many inter-specific matings are sterile or produce offspring that are infertile. Furthermore, if the individual is not sufficiently discriminating, it might mate with a mutant or deformed organism whose chance of procreating healthy individuals is slight. Such an event would terminate the gene line that the individual carries, eliminating such slack behavioral characteristics from the gene pool.

This mechanism, however, if promoted to extremes, would result in a reduction of genetic variability, or even incest with its attendant hazards and thus in the decline of the genes promoting it. As usual, long periods of pressure from natural selection has, in most species, produced a functional optimum in the form of preferential limits that are neither too wide, nor too narrow.

The Dangers of Incest

The danger of incestuous mating is that it increases the chance of offspring expressing recessive genetic defects when both its parents carry the me offending gene - as is most likely with closely related parents. A classic example of this is the fairly frequent occurrence of hemophilia in the scions of some highly interbred European royal families.

Because gene complements that allow incestuous mating would be less fit than those that opposed it, one might conclude that those genes directing their carriers to be repulsed by the concept of incest would survive in greater numbers than those that didn't, and that the former would become the norm. This seems to be the case with most animals.

To avoid incestuous relationships, however, an animal must be able to recognize its immediate kin. This is usually not possible for those individuals who have been raised apart from their parents and siblings, but since this seldom occurs under natural conditions, it is safe to assume that those individuals with whom one is intimate during infancy are in fact closely related and should be avoided as mates. Thus a gene complement can avoid incest by endowing its carrier with an emotional resistance toward mating with those individuals with whom it has had an intimate and prolonged childhood association.

Resistance to Incest in Humans

Research has shown that humans exhibit such a resistance and view those with whom they have had a close association before puberty as sexually undesirable. This research was carried out by Wolf [1] who investigated two cultures in which unrelated children of both sexes were raised together from an early age.

The first investigation concerned a village in China where it was the custom for the parents to choose a wife for a newborn son, usually before he was three years old. The prospective wife, also an infant, then left her own household to join that of the boy where they were raised as brother and sister until their wedding 10 to 15 years later. Not one of the several such unions he investigated was successful; all participants expressed deep dissatisfaction with the arrangements. Some rebelled and refused to be married; others acquiesced, but the husband quickly acquired a mistress.

The second investigation concerned children in Israeli kibbutzim who are raised in bisexual peer groups inhabiting common living and sleeping quarters until the third or fourth school grade. These individuals are not considered to be siblings, either by themselves, or by society and are therefore not constrained by any taboos towards incest. Yet several surveys have failed to reveal a single marriage or "even one love affair or one instance of publicly known sexual relations between members of the same peer group who were co-socialized from birth through most of their childhood." (quotation from Wolf).

An approach from a different angle was made by Weinberg[2], who, following a study of 37 instances of sibling incest in Chicago, concluded that in general the unions were transitory and the couples: "did not behave like marriage partners." There were, however, six exceptions in which the couples became mutually attached and contemplated marriage. In all the latter cases - and in only these cases - the brother and sister had been raised separately from early childhood.

It would appear, then, that the successful gene complement is one that instills in its carrier an aversion to mating with those individuals with whom it has been intimate during pre-puberty, since in this way the dangers of incest are avoided.

Selecting the Ideal Mate

As we have already noted, the attraction an individual feels towards a prospective mate is an important trait in itself, since to be successful, an individual must attempt to mate with a person showing the most promise. The individuals in a population who have proven to be most successful are those nearest the average in the most traits, since they are present in the largest numbers within the population - which is equivalent to success. Thus, the qualities to which an individual should be attracted in choosing a mate are those possessed by the members of the most successful reproductive age - which is, of course, early puberty. This is the reason that we are sexually attracted to those individuals displaying the average physical dimensions characteristic of mature youth.

Many qualities of an animal are not immediately obvious, however. For example, we are not aware of the immunological nature of most people we meet or of the presence of genetic faults they might be carrying. We therefore employ the only means open to us in judging the suitability of an individual as a mate, by observing her or his physical appearance.

We look first for the primary sexual characteristics and the age of people we meet to assess their reproductive prospects (i. e. whether they are neither too young nor too old). This is accompanied by an assessment of their vigor and health and the absence of deformities. Since physical injury or disease may result in deformities to the body and since these deformities seldom affect both sides of the body equally, symmetry is an important trait that we look for in choosing a healthy mate. Thus a successful individual is one who, not only possesses this trait, but who requires its presence in those it chooses to mate with.

Female Desirability

The age at which human females are considered to be most sexually desirable by their male counterparts, peaks shortly after puberty, since (as we have already observed) this is the age at which women's reproductive potential is at a maximum.

The male characteristic that responds to this appeal is probably itself a complex trait and therefore polygenetic. Thus, if quantified, the female age considered by males to be most attractive should peak in different males at different female ages.

For the male population as a whole, however, there would be a (probably somewhat skewed) distribution curve defining the proportion of the male population that considers each year in a female's life to be the most desirable. Thus a plot of this age, versus the percentage of the male population finding that age to be most desirable, would peak shortly after puberty and would tail off at ages greater and less than this maximum. Pedophiles would, therefore, be found amongst that fraction of the population occupying the lower tail of this curve.

Recent research has shown that human males of various races agree in general concerning the female facial features that they consider most desirable. As it turned out, these features proved to be near the average of each of several dimensions obtained from the measurements of a number of human female faces. Thus there seems to be a universal consensus as to what constitutes sexual desirability or beauty. Any individual who is either too fat or too thin, too tall or too short, or has any form of disability, is not usually considered to be sexually desirable.

In selecting a mate, the male faces another concern - the need to ascertain whether the female in whom he is interested is pregnant, since if she is, his efforts to reproduce will be frustrated. Early pregnancy is not obvious, but in time increasing weight and abdominal swelling signal this state. Thus it is that males of our species have a strong desire to impregnate slender females displaying a narrow waist and flat abdomen, since this is the surest indication available to the male that his prospective mate is not already impregnated. Large breasts and a broadened pelvic region are also of interest to the males since they serve as primary sex indicators and of their owner's suitability as a potential mother.

The male also finds the female's buttocks attractive. This attraction probably originated among his ancient predecessors who showed an interest in this female feature since it encouraged them to mount their mates abaft, and has probably been retained in today's males, as it continues to heighten their sexual desires.

Female Embellishment Industry

It is in the female's interest to attract as many males as she can, so as to provide as large a retinue as possible from which to make her selection. A successful female is therefore one who derives pleasure from increasing her sexual allure. This trait, or urge, serves to enrich those who are employed in the **female embellishment industry**, a major component of many societies whose function is to provide the cosmetics and attire required for this purpose.

Male Suitability

Women are attracted by such qualities as strength, virility and vigor, and find the appearance of social success to be sexually appealing. This is the reason that they tend to favor maturity in their mates and why their concept of male desirability peaks at a greater age than does female desirability. It probably also accounts for the fact that there are fewer female than male pedophiles in society.

Selective Mating is Itself a Trait Subject to Selection

The concept of the ideal mate is itself a trait - and being so, is subject to natural selection. It therefore exhibits biological variability in its nature and in the intensity with which it is expressed amongst individuals of a population - that is, not everyone's idea of beauty is precisely the same as everyone else's - and furthermore evolves as the population evolves so as always to correspond approximately to the population norms. We shall consider an example of this below.

Parental Direction of Mate Selection

As we saw earlier, in most societies, the parents assume a proprietorial interest in the reproductive functions of their children. This interest is vested mainly in their daughters, since women are potentially less able to produce as many offspring as men, and therefore have a greater investment in each birth than do their male siblings. Thus, there is an advantage in the genes promoting a tendency for the parents to impose their more mature judgment toward selection of a mate for their daughters. Influence is also exercised in the selection of their sons' mates, but is not considered as critical since the sowing of a few 'wild oats' can disperse the gene line more widely, and furthermore, are more readily concealed than similar unsanctioned acts performed by their daughters.

Foreplay

Another social activity exhibited by many primates, is grooming, which promotes bonding between the members of their groups. Humans do not partake of this activity but do engage in similar acts to demonstrate affection - such as hugging, kissing, and holding hands. This behavior in humans may be specified by a variation of the genes that promote grooming in other primates. In humans, however, this activity occurs with highest frequency between mating pairs, where it intensifies the pleasure, and hence the binding effectiveness, of the sexual union, taking the form of 'petting' and 'foreplay'.

The Formation of 'Mating Cliques'

There is another possible advantage for the genes of an organism to specify that its carrier possesses the desire to mate with individuals who are similar to itself, which is that the gene or gene complex will, by doing so, resist its own dilution in the gene pool as the population grows, and will maintain or even increase its own frequency. Consider a gene complex that calls for both specific visual markings on an animal and a desire in the animal to mate only with others having the same markings. These animals will form a mating clique whose members are protected from the dangers of unsuitable matings (as outlined above) and therefore have a slight advantage over non-members. As their frequency in the population grows, those having the desire but not the markings would find it harder and harder to obtain a willing mate, a situation that would lead to their ultimate demise. Those having the markings but not the discrimination would also disappear since they would continue to suffer the dangers posed by unsuitable mates.

We would, however, expect the anti-incest genes to continue to operate in the mating clique, just as they do in the general population, and to oppose a too stringent application of restrictive mating. This conflict between a desire to restrict mating, and at the same time to avoid incest, forges a population in which both drives are active in most individuals and therefore the resultant ratio between the intensity of these two drives will have a frequency that follows the usual distribution curve with an average, or functional optimum, corresponding to its peak intensity.

Genocentric Attraction

Sexual cliques form the nucleus around which many herds and flocks coalesce, with members of the clique occupying the center of the herd while the non-members are relegated to a more vulnerable position on the periphery. Since not to be a member of the clique threatens genetic oblivion, those individuals who strive (or have an emotional compulsion) to join the clique have a greater chance of survival. As a corollary then, not to be a member can be a frightening prospect. In modern human society the sexual clique has become the group of 'beautiful people' in which the majority of individuals desire membership. It is this desire that is so heavily exploited by the advertising and entertainment industries.

Genocentric attraction, or *the tendency to shun individuals who differ from us*, may also be the source of the emotional objection made by many towards attempts to alter the species by artificial means, such as eugenics and more recently, genetic engineering. After all, is a product of these activities (particularly the latter) whose genes have been altered, really one of US? There is also the rational objection, of course, that no one can define exactly what an improvement is - with the exception, of course, of the elimination of certain obvious genetically transmitted disabilities.

Other Aids to Mate Selection

Although we have used examples of visual signals serving as markers to promote restrictive mating, other types of markers serve as well. We have already seen that pheromones are frequently used, especially by insects, while many birds display elaborate mating rituals, showing that behavioral markers serve as well. Even plants can be found in which restrictive mating is practiced. Certain orchids attract, or physiologically restrict entry to their flowers to specific insects to ensure that those entering will carry only pollen from others of the same species.

Inherent Behavior is More Reliable Than Reasoned Behavior

This isn't to say that all behavior is inherent and that learning and reasoning have no influence on an animal's activities. But even for learning to be effective, certain behavioral patterns may be required. Take, for example, the teaching of hunting to young predators by experienced animals. Here, tolerance on the part of the older animal is required since it must allow the younger one to accompany it during the hunt. The apprentice for its part, must not only have the desire to learn, but must be both submissive and attentive during the lesson. To entrust such important behavior to the intelligence of the two participants would be too risky, and I hereby affirm as a generality, that no matter what behavior a species employs to enhance its fitness, *behavior must be inherent to guarantee success under a majority of situations.* This is an important affirmation and will be basic to many of the arguments presented in the remainder of this work.

References
1. Wolf, Arthur P. 1966. Childhood Association, Sexual Attraction, and the Incest Taboo. American Anthropologist 68:883-98.

2. Weinberg, K.S. Incest behavior New York: Citadel Press. 1963.

CHAPTER FIVE

SOME THOUGHTS ON THINKING

Even the most primitive animals must be capable of responding to conditions in their environment that affect their welfare. To do so requires that they are able, first to detect the conditions that are of concern to them, and second to act in such a way as to profit from this information. Contact with their environment is made through **sensors**, which *quantify such conditions as temperature, light intensity, touch, sound, and the presence of specific chemical compounds*. With the information supplied by their sensors, they must then decide whether a response is necessary and if so, what that response is to be. The reaction of the more primitive animals, such as the paramecium, is simply to move away from regions in which conditions are adverse and toward localities in which conditions are favorable. The same applies to multi-cellular animals, but in this case, due to the complexity and size of the animal, a **nervous system** consisting of three basic types of elements - sensors, decision-making apparatuses and effectors, is required.

We cannot be sure how the most primitive nervous systems were constructed, since the organisms that possessed them are now extinct, along with 99.9 percent of all the species that have ever existed. The nervous systems of even the simplest of animals alive today, are fairly complex and cannot have evolved in a single mutation. We can, however, assume that the more complex systems could have been selected through a series of small changes, each of which must, of course, have conferred some advantage on the individuals possessing them over others that did not.

For three and a half billion years, after starting with the simplest life form, this mundane process (natural selection) slowly wove its intricate fabric, culminating in the most complex biological construct of all - **the human brain!**

The Incredible Complexity of the Human Brain!

The human brain is a bundle of communicating nerve cells, which are connected to each other to form a network of incredible intricacy. These connections, termed **synapses**, control the movement of nervous impulses by inhibiting or promoting their movement between the cells.

The complexity of the human brain is beyond even its own powers of comprehension. It has been estimated that there could be as many as 10^{14} (one hundred million million) synapses packed into this relatively small organ.

How does this compare with the modern computer?

Assuming that a synapse is roughly equivalent to a transistor, it would require 10 million personal computers, each containing ten million (10^7) transistors, to match the number of switches present in a single human brain! The fact is, however, that the synapse is not a simple switch, but is a complex organelle in its own right, containing a number of ion channels and multiple points of control. Furthermore, combining 10 million processors in a configuration with a logic power the equal of the human brain is well beyond our present capabilities!

The astonishing fact is, however, that at the time of conception, the information necessary to construct this inconceivably complex organ (as well as all the rest of the trillion or so cells in the human body) is contained in the chromosomes - a volume less than a millionth of a cubic millimeter!

How this amazing structure furnishes us with **consciousness**, with a memory, with the ability to reason, to plan our activities and to control the movements of our bodies, is well beyond our present powers of comprehension. We shall, therefore, in the following discourse, consider only some of the peripheral features of the enormous power which the human brain possesses. Thus, in spite of the fact that we do not know how it works, we can still make some generalizations about its product - our thoughts.

Conceptual Thinking

Immanual Kant argued that the human mind possesses *a priori* concepts of time and space - or that we are born with spacial and temporal frameworks into which to fit our experiences. In fact, not only are space and time conceptual, but our whole mode of thinking is basically conceptual. Thus, in addition to the *a priori* concepts - or **preconcepts** - with which we are all born, throughout our lives we are constantly forming new concepts. These are essential, not only in allowing us to think and to remember, but also to communicate with others.

As an example of a new, or learned concept, consider that of a 'chair'. The object we perceive as a chair can take thousands of forms, yet we have little trouble identifying such an object, even when we see it in an elaborate form new to us. This results from the fact that we all have the general concept 'chair' fixed in our minds. Because of this, we all agree that a chair usually has four legs, a seat and a back. However, the variations on this theme are enormous. It may or may not have armrests; it may have a pedestal rather than legs; it may be upholstered or bare; it may be firm or on rockers or wheels. Although its most important feature is essentially utilitarian - to support a single person in a sitting position (a purely subjective requirement), we still recognize it in a miniature form (a doll's chair) into which no human could possibly fit. On the other hand, there are restrictions to our concept of a chair - for example, it must have a back - otherwise it is a stool - and it cannot have room for more than one person, since then it would be a bench or a couch.

How could we program a computer to recognize a chair in all the forms we readily accept? Any attempt to define a universal chair, if too detailed, would inevitably exclude some of the accepted forms. On the other hand, too loose a definition would have the computer including objects we ourselves would not include in the category 'chair'. To us a chair is not only an object with a specific form, but with a specific function as well.

Plato would probably have said that such an object possesses the essential quality of 'chairness', and that the mind recognizes this quality in the object, just as it recognizes the quality of 'beauty' in other objects. I would suggest, however, that the mind, by ascribing this quality to the object, forms a concept of a 'chair'. This appears to be an essential feature of the mind - to abstract certain features of an object so that it can categorize it, thus simplifying the process of recording and manipulating the images of the multitude of objects we encounter in our lives.

Conceptual Thinking is Inexact - but It Works!

Conceptual thinking is an essentially inaccurate process, but functions very well in communicating with others. This is so, because we all have a very clear idea of what our concepts mean. In fact they are very real to us. When examined closely, however, we find they are quite inexact. For example, if I say to you that I will meet you at the top of that hill (to which I point) at noon, there is no question in your mind what I mean since we both understand the concept of a 'hill', its 'top', of 'noon', and of the process of 'meeting'. Thus, at the agreed time and place, we will come together, perhaps not in physical contact, but close enough to each other that we may communicate comfortably - which we both understand to be the meaning of 'meeting'.

But if we were to examine these concepts and try to decide what exactly constitutes the 'hill' we are standing on, could either of us be certain where its boundaries are, or where the exact 'top' of the hill is located, or even how close we must be before we can say that we have 'met'? The time, 'noon', we might argue, is precisely defined by astronomers. Is it indeed? How long does it last? If we specify this time of duration as being a second, for example, we are then stating that noon lasts from half a second before noon to half a second past noon - an obvious absurdity! Perhaps we can solve the problem by specifying a shorter time interval - a microsecond for example - but our enigma still exists. The answer a mathematician would give, is 'for a vanishingly short time' - (another concept) that is to say that it is never exactly noon. Thus we see that any attempt to define our concepts too accurately results in absurdities!

There is no such thing as exact time, or absolute coordinates of space, yet we all have firmly established concepts of both these non-entities. The important thing is, however, that it is the universal possession of these, and similar concepts, that makes communication between us possible.

The 'Perfect' State Is Only One of an Infinity of States

Ideality or **perfection** are common concepts, in which we select one specific state of the universe - out of the infinite number of states that could exist - simply because, to us, this state is most desirable. 'Perfect health', for example, is a specific configuration of the atoms composing our bodies, but again it is only one such configuration out of the infinite number possible.

It is interesting to note, however, that because we have a concept of 'perfect health' together with the desire and ability to attain it, the probability of its occurrence is multiplied by an astronomical factor.

Are We Misled by Our Concepts?

The fact that we are dealing with approximations, you might say, is a triviality. The problem is, however, that if our concepts do not reveal to us the exact truth, might we not be fooled by them under certain circumstances, especially since we are so convinced of their truth? For example, it was commonly thought that the earth was flat and that, like all other 'flat surfaces' with which people were acquainted, must have an 'edge'. Humans possessed the preconcepts of 'up' and 'down' - which they were convinced were absolutes - leading to the conclusion that if one were not careful, one could fall off the edge of the world! Similarly, to the ancients, it was 'obvious' that the earth stood 'still' and that the sun 'revolved' around it. So strongly were they convinced of this 'fact', that the suggestion that this was not so was considered dangerous and was met with hostility.

As another example - our *a priori* concept, or preconception, of space, convinces us that it stretches away from us uniformly in all directions without limit. The idea that modern physicists have been forced to accept, is that space is curved back on itself and is therefore finite in extent rather than infinite. This is very difficult for most of us to accept since it violates our 'natural' instincts (or preconceptions), which we find easier to accept, and which prompts us to ask the question: "Yes, but if space is just a big ball, what's outside it?"

We also have a similar fixation with the concept of 'time', which we see as flowing like a river at a constant rate from an infinite past to an infinite future. Matter, on the other hand, since it is assumed to be subject to the law of cause and effect - that is, since every event is the result of, or was caused by, one specific previous event - may not have existed for all time, and therefore there must have been a **first cause**. Thus by assigning this first cause to 'God', we can accept that before the creation of matter there existed a 'void', which we have no trouble in visualizing as a huge empty space existing in infinite time, and in which God, Who has also existed since the infinite past, performs the miracle of creating matter at certain particular coordinates of space and time.

A more reasoned view - that space and time can have no meaning or existence without matter, since it is events (which cannot occur in the absence of matter) that define both space and time - is incomprehensible to us. We cannot accept that if space and time are coexistent with matter, then matter must have existed for all time, and we are forced by our preconceptions - when confronted by this suggestion - to ask the question: "Yes, but what happened before the beginning of time?" Thus the idea that the entire cosmos, including space and time, began in an instant during 'the big bang' is not easy to accept.

Cause, Effect and Quantum Mechanics

Even the principle of cause and effect itself has been thrown into doubt. Most people at the turn of the century held this principle to be self-evident. Physicists declared that all the laws of nature were understood except for a few minor inconsistencies, which would disappear as we increased the accuracy of our measurements, allowing us to predict events exactly. However, in attempting to trim off these errant threads, the fabric of nineteenth-century science was irrevocably torn! Scientists were forced to accept that at the fundamental level of particle-particle interactions, events by their very nature were determined by chance. Thus it was shown that there is an inherent indeterminacy in the parameters of any physical system, and furthermore, the magnitude of this uncertainty can be estimated by a simple expression arising from Heisenberg's uncertainty principle. This means that we cannot predict precisely the outcome of an event, such as the collision of two fundamental particles, but can only assign probabilities to each of a number of possible courses that subsequent events might follow.

This is the outcome of the field of study known as **quantum mechanics**, which came into being in the early twentieth century. Before 1900, physics was based on the laws of motion established mainly by Isaac Newton. These laws simply quantified the knowledge that even the most primitive human knew intuitively as he hurled his first spear - compensating for the effect of wind and gravity as he did so. Because of their intuitive nature we have had little trouble in accepting Newton's laws.

However, in the early part of the last century, Albert Einstein extended and modified Newton's laws by introducing the concept of 'relativity'. Since these modifications did not apply to everyday experience, but rather to the universe of cosmic dimensions and velocities, they were less intuitive and therefore less easy to accept. But not even Einstein was prepared to accept the indeterminacy that the proposals of quantum theory introduce shortly afterward, even though his own Nobel prize-winning contributions helped to provide the basis for this theory. This led to his well-known declaration that: "God does not play dice (with the universe)!"

Our approach to quantum mechanics is based on two simple but familiar concepts of how energy can be transmitted through space and time: the first, as a solid object (such as a bullet) hurtling through space, and the second, as ripples on the surface of a pond. These concepts, naive as they are, have led to the derivation of the highly predictive **Schroedinger equation**. Subatomic particles use neither of these processes individually, however, but rather, both at once! Since this is foreign to our everyday experiences, physicists have been unable to combine these ideas into a single unifying concept, which has induced the perceptive physicist, Richard Feynman to lament, that: "Nobody really understands quantum mechanics!"

Today we have to deal with an even more bizarre consequence of Heisenberg's uncertainty principle. The possibility has been recognized that it would not contravene natural laws for particles to appear spontaneously in empty space (that is, without apparent cause) - the only requirement being that the duration of this appearance not exceed a time interval specified by the uncertainty principle. These particles, which do not 'exist' in the usual meaning of the word, are referred to as 'virtual' particles. Thus empty space may be viewed as a cloud of such particles, which, despite their evanescence, are able to affect changes in the 'real' world. The implication of this possibility is, that there was not a single first cause, but that first causes are universal, constant and continuing phenomena throughout the cosmos. Perhaps the truth is, that while the principle of cause and effect applies accurately to the macro-world, as we consider smaller and smaller dimensions, this accuracy declines, ultimately vanishing as the dimensions approach zero.

Is the Universe Multi-Dimensional?

As another example of our limitations, we are convinced by our preconception of space that the universe is three-dimensional and while we can think and act very well in three dimensions, we are unable to visualize a universe of four or more dimensions - yet the universe may be multi-dimensional. We have a tendency to assume that there cannot be other dimensions simply because we are not aware of them, but in fact there is no reason to suppose that the number of dimensions defining the universe has any limit! Were the universe of such a multi-dimensional nature, it is obvious that we could never 'understand' it in the usual sense, since we do not possess the necessary preconceptions. We need only attempt to visualize a four-dimensional space to appreciate the futility of it!

The Mind is a Blunt Instrument

The reason we do not have multi-dimensional preconcepts is, obviously, that we live and operate adequately in three-dimensional space. Thus, during the major part of our evolutionary history, nothing would have been gained by possessing concepts beyond this limit. We also function well in dealing with objects whose size roughly matches that of our own. It may be, however, that in attempting to apply our concepts to the realm of subatomic dimensions and of cosmic proportions, we are extrapolating beyond our capabilities. Thus, while conceptual thinking allows us to deal extremely well with the Newtonian universe - that is, the world of our dimensional scale - we are ill equipped to 'comprehend' that of Heisenberg or Einstein! Perhaps the naked human mind is simply too blunt an instrument to dissect such an intricate multi-dimensional universe, which is therefore beyond our comprehensional powers.

Concepts - Signposts on a Featureless Landscape

We see, then, that we are compelled to function in a world that appears to have no boundaries - where all things grade into other things as the side of the valley grades into the side of the hill. Even that paragon of concrete symmetry, the billiard ball, if sufficiently enlarged, would be found to be rougher than the earth. Its 'surface', we now know, consists of an irregular layer of molecules in constant motion, making it impossible for us to specify exactly where this object starts or stops. In playing the game of billiards, however, we operate at a larger scale where this information is of no consequence, and we can play the game perfectly well with the assumption that each ball corresponds exactly to our concept of a 'perfect sphere'. The success of the game relies on the fact that the imperfections in the balls and table top are insignificant compared to the limitations in the skill of even the most expert player.

Evolution has, as usual, resulted in the selection of a most practical mechanism for dealing with the problem of perceiving an essentially relative universe, by providing us with a number of reference points - our concepts. There is no question that this has been of immense benefit to us in the matter of survival in a universe that shows no particular concern for our welfare. It does not necessarily follow, however, that a mind selected in this way is equipped to answer all the questions it might put to itself!

Let us not despair at our limitations, however, but instead begin by recognizing them, then proceed, using our ingenuity to function within our limits, just as we have done so successfully in dealing with the quantum world. Here, analogy has been extremely useful, and might again be employed in considering a multi-dimensional universe in which mass and electric charge, for example, are treated as dimensions orthogonal to all three space axes. In this case we would recognize that, although we are unable to perceive these quantities directly as dimensions, we are nevertheless aware of their vectorial components projected into our three-dimensional space. Thus, by analogy, we could treat them as we do three dimensional vectors, which we resolve by projection onto two dimensional planes.

Many of our concepts also evoke positive or negative feelings. The intensity of these feelings that each concept evokes will vary, however, in accordance with the nature of any previous experiences we may associate with the concept. This is particularly true of our feelings towards various persons, whom we may intensely *love* or *hate*, or merely *like* or *dislike*. Furthermore, we are, at times unconsciously biased towards others we have newly met, especially if they resemble persons with whom we are more familiar. This results from the attempt of the mind to categorize objects and people during the formation of new concepts.

Learning

There is no doubt that first impressions are lasting, but our total concept of an object is certainly not immutable. For example, we may have only seen a rubber ball without handling it on our first encounter and not have been aware of its 'softness'. This may come to our attention on further encounters with it at which time our concept of it is deepened by the realization of its other qualities.

Learning, then, is *the process of forming new concepts, which are defined in terms of older or more 'familiar' ones.* Essentially what our minds do, is to classify new information in terms of older familiar categories. When examining a new object, we look first for familiar qualities. Our first impression of a billiard ball is that it has a spherical shape, which we confirm by looking at it from several angles. This we do because our concept of 'spherical' evokes the concept of 'symmetry'. On further examination of this new object by touch, however, we note that, unlike the rubber ball, it is 'hard' and 'smooth'.

Since these associations are made through experience, they vary between individuals - and even in the same individual, they vary over time. Thus an individual familiar with, but unskilled in the game of billiards, when asked to separate a billiard ball from a number of other objects would have little trouble in rejecting anything that is either too large or too small or has an irregular shape. With even an elementary knowledge of the game, one would realize that the billiard ball's most important quality is its ability to follow a 'perfectly straight' line when rolling across a 'flat surface', and therefore it could be tested accordingly. A more experienced person, however, would test it still further by observing it in collision with another ball, since her or his concept of the billiard ball is that it possesses a certain 'resilience'.

Preconcepts - Concepts We Inherit

Learning, as we have noted, is the process of forming new concepts, which are defined in terms of older or more familiar ones. It is therefore essentially relative - the idea that knowledge can be 'absolute' is without foundation.

Where does such a process begin? Here again the answer has evolved through natural selection, in the form of inherited (*a priori*) concepts, or preconcepts. These are not present in the mind of the newly born as fully developed concepts but are, rather, predispositions to view the world in a specific way - a sort of guide to the nascent mind. Thus, we may think of the brain as a vessel and the mind as its contents. The composition of the contents may vary, but their shape is determined by that of the vessel. Similarly, the shape, or physiology of the brain is inherited, and with it a conceptual spacial and temporal framework into which the infant fits its experiences and organizes its knowledge concerning the world.

The preconceptions with which we are born are not complete but must be developed, or defined, through experience. Such defining has been termed **imprinting**, the most famous example of which is that described by Lorenz who found that young ducks and goslings became 'imprinted' upon their mothers, whom they would subsequently follow to food and away from danger. Lorenz showed that the young could be imprinted on a number of other objects, including himself, which they encounter following birth. These birds apparently were born with an urge to follow and become attached to the first object they observed in motion upon emerging from their eggs. Since the mother was usually guarding the nest at the time, this urge served to ensure that their attachment was made to her. We might say that the young were born with the concept of an 'object providing security', which had to be defined, and was, as the first object they saw in motion.

The Self and Other Persons

There are a number of *a priori* concepts, or preconceptions other than space and time, which are vital to our survival. Probably the most important such concept is that of the **self**. Another is 'object', or 'thing', or 'concrete entity'. Thus the very young infant experiences stimulations to its optic nerve, some of which appear to change, or to 'move'. (Detecting movement is another concept that appears to be an essential part of brain function since it has been shown to be associated with specific neurons and is therefore probably inherited as a preconception). Gradually the child will realize that these sensations have a certain 'coherence', or that they move together or are 'grouped' as 'objects'. It will not, of course, realize immediately the concrete nature of these objects, or that they exist in 'space'. Next it will be aware that there are certain sensations associated with the movement of certain objects - as when its arm involuntarily moves through its field of vision - but not others, and that its own thoughts can cause movements of those objects with which these sensations are associated. Ultimately it realizes that certain afferent and efferent neural impulses can be combined into a single concept - the 'self'. And so its universe is divided into two parts - one containing objects that are part of itself and the other, containing objects that are not.

Through the use of its hands, probably among the first objects it associates with itself, it is able to explore and to develop the concept of space. It will become familiar with the fact that it cannot extend its arm to touch all objects that it sees and eventually it will come to associate the complex neurological impulses with the ability to reach and ultimately to grasp and manipulate various objects. In this process the sense of touch will play an essential role since through it a concept of the 'concrete' or 'impenetrable' nature of objects will be formed, as opposed to the 'yielding' nature of others, such as 'water'.

Once the concept of 'self' is established, further concepts can be formed or defined in terms of the self. 'Space' is, of course, one of the most important of these. 'Time' follows from the realization that events occur in sequence. The existence of 'mother' and of other 'people' or 'persons' similar to, but separate from, the self, form new concepts. Most subjective concepts are established using the greatest teachers of all - pleasure and pain. Thus most concepts have an emotional content, since they are associated with either pleasure or pain, or with the promotion of gratification or frustration, and therefore possess either a positive or negative connotation.

Learning Equals Familiarization or Association

Most concepts are not inherited, however, but are probably formed *de nova* through experience. We term this 'learning', which we have stated is the process of categorizing new information in terms of previously established 'familiar' concepts, (or associating the 'new' with the 'old') so that we may 'understand' them. Each concept may in time, as a result of experience, come to be associated with other concepts. The concept 'smooth', for example, has tactile connotations since we tend to draw our fingers across a surface to determine whether it is smooth. Experience has also taught us that light is frequently reflected from smooth surfaces so that we tend to associate 'smoothness' with 'shiny'. Throughout our lives we are constantly making such associations, causing us to qualify many of our older concepts and to form new ones, which we define in terms of the more familiar ones. Because of this, our concepts are very personal, depending on the sum total of our own individual experiences. It is little wonder, therefore, that few of us are in complete agreement with others as to the exact meaning of all our concepts.

Absolute Knowledge is a Fiction

The indeterminate nature of conceptual thinking means that, in essence, we view the universe through a narrow slit - or a distorted window - and that therefore 'knowledge' can never be 'absolute' or even 'ultimate'. We can only approximate to reality. For example, we consider that our knowledge was enormously increased by the discovery that matter consists of atoms, and was further advanced by introducing the concept of 'fundamental' particles constituting atoms, but are these 'real', or simply highly successful and readily visualized concepts - ones that allow us to make accurate predictions?

But in spite of the fact that conceptual thinking is approximate and far from immutable, it allows us to communicate with each other and to function very well in a complex universe. There is little doubt of the survival value of this kind of thought process. It has been selected for, simply because - *it works*!

The Mechanism of Conceptual Thought

How are Concepts Stored and Elicited in the Brain?

One possibility is that they are retained within the brain in neural structures, nodes or centers, which, when stimulated, instead of issuing commands directly to a muscle or other effector as most stimuli do, inject concepts into our chain of thought' or consciousness.

As an example, when we hear the words 'rubber ball', the appropriate neural center is stimulated to evoke a visual image of this object. But since we have encountered it before, our previous experience has caused us to associate certain qualities with it by forming neural links to other centers, which in turn inject other concepts into our consciousness, reminding us that this object is 'smooth', 'round' and 'soft', or 'yielding'.

Thus, the process of hearing or reading the words: "rubber ball" triggers activity in one center, which in turn stimulates others through connections made on our previous encounters with the object. This is a form of memory, since what our mind has done, is to abstract certain features of the object that impressed us during previous encounters, and stored them to be recalled on subsequent interactions with the same object.

The episode in which we examined the rubber ball is now fixed in our memory by the formation of a neural center with connections to other centers denoting its qualities. Upon subsequently being reminded of this object, the specific center with which it is associated is stimulated and in turn stimulates all the other centers to which it is connected. The result of all this activity is that our conscious thoughts become aware of the concept of an object fused with the concepts of the qualities that impressed us during our previous experiences with it. To the mind, the object is the sum of its qualities. We do not consciously enumerate these qualities each time we look at an object, yet they influence our concept of it. One might say, that like food, we are conscious of its 'taste' without being aware of all the individual 'flavors' contributed by the ingredients that make it up.

What Is the Origin of Our 'Stream of Consciousness'?
This view of our thought processes suggests that our stream of consciousness consists of a chain of stimulated centers; each center, when stimulated, not only generates a pattern of impulses, evoking a specific concept in our conscious thoughts, but in turn stimulates other centers. In this way, our previous encounters with the object are recreated by a process that is essentially a reversal of the original process in which our impressions of the object were abstracted and stored. These stored impressions are now called forth to evoke in us the same impressions or feelings we experienced during previous meetings with the object.

During the original encounter, the brain is inundated by a sea of external impulses provided by the senses. The mind cannot possibly absorb these impulses in their entirety, but rather abstracts the more prominent few and stores them in memory in the form of concepts. During recall the brain seeks to reproduce the effect of the original deluge by supplying the same essential impulses to the consciousness, but this time their origin is internal. Stimulation of the centers storing the original concepts is the mechanism by which recall is achieved.

Such chains are constantly being initiated, interrupted or diverted by external stimuli arriving from our senses - objects we see - sounds we hear, such as words or loud noises. These evoke other images and feelings, starting other chains of thought coursing through the complex interconnections between the neural centers in our brains.

As we view a scene, our senses send an enormous amount of information to the brain in the form of a continuous stream of neural impulses. The brain, however, as we have seen, does not store all of this information but appears to abstract salient features - usually referred to as 'impressions' - which are recorded as far as possible, in terms of familiar concepts. We can experience this operation by attempting to recall a room that we may have visited briefly at some time in the recent past. We will find that we are aware of few details - such as the pattern of the wall paper, or the pictures on the wall, unless they were drawn to our attention at the time - in spite of the fact that our eyes may have provided details of every square centimeter of the walls, floor, ceiling and contents.

On the other hand, we will have retained specific impressions (concepts) of the appearance of the room, and be able to recall such facts as - was it 'cold' and 'clinical', like a room in a hospital - or did it feel 'warm' and 'inviting'; was it 'large' or 'small'; where were the doors and windows located? We may remember certain pieces of furniture - perhaps a chair we sat in, or a table we bumped into - but more likely we have only an impression as to the amount of furniture present, i.e., was it 'cluttered' or 'bare'? These are all familiar concepts that the mind uses in establishing a new concept of a room that we have only seen once but whose 'image' we feel is retained in our memory. Now, when we recall the scene, all these concepts are re-injected into our consciousness, repeating, not the detailed picture we first saw, but the salient features that were abstracted at the moment of viewing, and in this way, rebuilding the overall initial impression or feelings we had - or, in effect, causing us, once again, to 'experience' our encounter with the room.

Thus, the use of established concepts to categorize and store information provides the mind with an economical means of recording the essentials of past events.

What Is the Storage Capacity of the Brain?

The eye has a time resolution of somewhat less than a tenth of a second; that is, it is unable to recognize, as an individual event, any action whose duration is less than an interval of this order. If we take this to be true of the brain in general, we could record our entire life history by using units of tenths of seconds as **moments**, and recording the condition of each synapse present in the brain during that moment . This is impossible, of course, since it would require all our synapses to record one moment of brain function and leave none for subsequent intervals. However, we do not remember the details of every moment of our lives - rather, only a very small fraction of all the moments of our lives are committed to long term memory, and as I have indicated, through the use of conceptual thinking, even those that are retained, are retained in an abstracted form, which is to say that the status of only a small fraction of synapses need be recorded to provide an impression of each moment.

In a lifetime of 100 years, there would be approximately 3×10^{10} (thirty billion) moments, allowing 3000 synapses to record each single moment of life. However, only very rarely do we remember each incident moment by moment, as, for example, when we recall a conversation 'word for word', instead of simply remembering the 'gist' of what was said. Thus, it is probable that less than a millionth of all the moments of our lives are remembered, which, if true, would allow 3 billion synapses to handle each recorded moment. All the brain is not used as storage for information, however, since information processing - the part of the brain that abstracts the information, decides what is to be retained and allows us to recall it in the future - will demand a large portion of neuronal function, as will also the motor centers controlling body movement and the sensory processing mechanisms. But even if memory employs only a third of the available neurons, the number of synapses involved in this function is still impressive.

Is There Really a 'Me'?

Each of us tends to believe that there must be an over-seer or control center in our brain that is really 'me', but must there be? Could the stream of stimulated nodes making up our **consciousness** not itself be self-propagating, modulated by input from our surroundings? With millions of nerves from all parts of our bodies constantly flooding the brain with stimuli, one thought, and one thought only must dominate - but only temporarily - yielding quickly to its successor and providing us with what we experience as our 'stream of consciousness'. Each thought cannot be preordained by its immediate predecessor since thinking does not inevitably follow the same line. Instead it arises as a result of a particular combination - not only of previously dominant nodes - but of other more subtle forces, such as mood and emotions which we will consider later. Perhaps **free will** is an illusion and the variety of responses we exhibit arises by chance from the incredibly complex nature of the brain and from the enormous amount of information constantly being fed into it. Our conscious thoughts, or 'consciousness', may only be the ripples on the surface of a turbulent pool - an integration or modulation of millions upon millions of stimulus spikes.

Two Modes of Thought

Our consciousness occupies the middle ground between inner and outer stimuli. We can operate in either an introspective or externally sensitive mode - although not exclusively in either. In the externally sensitive phase, we concentrate on stimuli originating in the outside world, which are sifted and abstracted - while during introspection, stimuli are generated internally. These two modes of operation of the mind are not mutually exclusive, however. While absorbing new information, we are constantly attempting to search through our stored concepts for familiarity; to remember to whom that face belongs, for example, by characterizing it and comparing its overall qualities to those stored as concepts of persons we know. So too, even in our deepest reverie or introspective mood we are aware and can become aroused by strong external stimuli, such as loud sounds or a sudden movement.

Moods

The incredible complexity of the brain is responsible for the deeper feelings, or 'moods' we experience. These depend on whether the preponderance of stimulated nodes or concepts at any moment has a positive or negative connotation. Our mood is *joyful* and we feel *happy* if a large number of our active concepts are positive, or *sad* and *depressed* if mainly negative centers are operating.

Beliefs are ***convictions that the urges and goals we seek are important, genuine, or even absolute.*** Furthermore, they make us *want* to accept these goals, since such a desire heightens their effectiveness and, as a result, the success of the genes specifying them. We shall see how important this is in convincing us to become active members of a social group by submitting to its authority which, in turn, we personify as 'God' or 'the Nation'.

Memories are stored in the rational mind as concepts to be recalled as required and injected into the individual's stream of consciousness. We see then, that the two parts off the mind are intimately connected by a number of neural links.

To summarize...
In summary then: the memory of an episode may simply be a record of a string of concepts, which, when activated, inject the 'feelings' and 'impressions' experienced during the actual event into our present consciousness in a repetition of the original sequence. Thus, as the neural centers are the building blocks of our brains, **concepts are the building blocks of our mind** and can be used repeatedly in evaluating and abstracting current events, committing them to memory and regenerating the events in our consciousness in essentially the same abstracted form they originally took.

Speech

The function of the mind to abstract, to categorize, to form concepts - is absolutely basic to its operation. Furthermore, without conceptual thought, it is unlikely that speech would have evolved, since **speech** is, in part at least, ***the process of giving nomenclature to our concepts in order to communicate with others whose concepts and nomenclature agree more or less with our own.*** (For a list of many - but not all - of the concepts held by human beings, consult a dictionary).

Perhaps our brains evolved using concepts as the basic unit of thought since evolution in this direction made speech possible and provided a considerable advantage to those members of our species having this capability. Another possibility (which I personally consider more likely) is that speech resulted *because* our minds already functioned in this way, having evolved, as we have postulated, as a multi-centered organ. In any case, it is likely that speech and an increasing ability to conceptualize - an essential component of intelligence - evolved together.

It is interesting to note that we both communicate, and think, in a linear manner. In fact, we might say that in thinking we are essentially communicating with ourselves. While speaking a second language, we sometimes think in terms of the first, then translate to the second language before speaking. It is much more efficient, however, to think in the language one is speaking. All these facts point out the strong parallelism between speaking and conceptual thought.

The Physiology of Speech.

Speech, however, is much more complicated than simply giving nomenclature to our concepts - this is only the first step. The single concepts must next be combined using the rules of grammar into larger concepts, or sentences. These, in turn, are transferred to certain motor areas of the brain that command the vocal apparatus, causing it to articulate the words and issue them as sounds. The listener's ears, upon receiving the sound waves, transform them into nerve stimuli. These are fed to another region of the brain whose function it is to convert them into a form that will elicit the concepts specified by the words and inject them into the consciousness of the listener. This is an immensely complex system, which evolved in a relatively short time by evolutionary standards, indicating that the species must have been under very great stress - a fact that we will consider below.

Although we are able to communicate simple concepts through speech, the real challenge the speaker - or writer - faces, is to communicate the more abstract concepts, or thoughts, for which there are no individual words.

Speech and the Formation of Societies

The development of speech made more complex, and effective societies possible. One might draw an analogy here, noting that speech is to society what the nervous system is to the individual. Not only does it coordinate society's actions, but provides it with a memory as well.

For societies to function optimally, however, it was first necessary that we evolve appropriate attitudes and behavior, which we now refer to as 'morality' or 'ethics', subjects we will consider presently. Before doing so, however, we must consider how the goals we seek have evolved - and this will form the subject of our next chapter.

CHAPTER SIX

EVOLUTION OF SOCIETY

It Pays To Be Gregarious

Homo sapiens evolved in a relatively short time by comparison with the usual evolutionary changes. Such speed suggests intense selective pressures, since most successful species will remain unchanged unless threatened by a challenge from a specific direction. In the case of humans, this pressure probably came originally from the usual animal predators, but as the population increased, the main threat faced by most human tribes would probably have been that arising from competition with other tribes.

In such a competitive world, the possibility of survival of an individual living alone would be very small. Even a family on its own would find life precarious since the loss of one or both parents would mean almost certain death for the young, and, as a result, the destruction of the gene line of the parents. This became increasingly so as the species evolved a more complex nature, requiring a longer period for the young to develop to maturity, and hence a longer period of dependent childhood. For this reason it became crucial for individuals to join a stable group or tribe, not only for their own immediate safety, but also to increase the probability that their descendants would survive to continue their gene line should either or both parents die before their offspring reached maturity.

Thus an advantage would have accrued to those individuals who associated to form a union with others whom they believed could be trusted to support them and, should they die, their families as well.

This means that, for the survival of the individuals and the genes they carry, the genes must endow the individual who carries them (the carrier) with **gregariousness** - *an inherent desire to join and remain with a group or tribe*. One might argue that this needn't be an urge since it should be obvious to the individual and would therefore become a tradition through parental instruction. Communal living, however, was likely practiced by man's very early, and less intelligent precursors, in whom an urge to stay close to their fellows would be more reliable than a reasoned decision to do so, just as with herding animals. Those having this natural urge would have a greater chance of survival and would therefore have increased in numbers relative to those who did not, which is why we find that **gregariousness** is a common behavioral trait in most humans today.

It Pays To Associate With Altruists

There is little doubt that the best interests of the individual (and the individual's gene complement) would be served by joining a group of **altruists** - *those who would be dedicated to the protection, not only of the individuals joining them, but of the latter's offspring as well*. Such an idealistic group would be unstable, however, since it would be extremely vulnerable to **cheaters** - *individuals who would only pretend to be reliable while exploiting the naive.* Cheaters would inevitably, either invade the group from outside, or arise within the group simply due to the biological variability in the degree of the reliability or altruistic trait versus the 'selfish' trait. Once established within a society, cheaters would flourish, since their offspring would enjoy the protection of the naive, while the descendants of the latter would be neglected or even destroyed. This would eventually lead to the elimination of the altruistic genes and the formation of a tribe of cheaters - a society that in its turn would disintegrate as each member sought to take advantage of their fellow members without themselves contributing to the welfare of the group.

It Pays To Be Skeptical

The destruction of an altruistic society could be prevented, however, if each of its members possessed another quality or trait that we might term **skepticism**. This is *an emotional or inherent urge that compels its possessor to be constantly on the alert for cheaters, and to avoid associating with them once they have been discovered.* Egoism and gregariousness are two qualities that cause individuals to seek out others who may be trusted to protect them and their families, while skepticism compels them to eschew those who would not do so. In fact, the threat that the untrustworthy pose to the gene line is so great that only genes stipulating an instantaneous repulsion of those perceived to be treacherous by its carrier, could survive.

All life is directed towards one important goal - *to exploit its environment without itself being exploited.* Promoting our ability to resist exploitation is the reason that skepticism is so important to us, since it provides us with the urge to beware of hazards posed by those on whom we must rely for our own welfare.

There is little doubt that this trait is common in modern humans, since most of us are aware that upon meeting other people for the first time, we instinctively attempt to assess their character, while at the same time being conscious that we ourselves are under scrutiny. What each of us is attempting to do is to determine the reliability of the other, since if the other person is trustworthy, then we are safe in giving her or him our loyalty, or to accept that person as 'one of us'. On the other hand, if we feel that our new acquaintance does not warrant our trust, we will in future tend to avoid her or him.

We are, in effect, establishing a concept of persons we have just met by combining all our impressions of them. Our concern is whether they constitute a threat to us or not. If our immediate impression is that they are different from us in any way and therefore not one of us, we feel that we must be wary, or at least reserved. Initially we make such decisions by observing other people's physical appearance and demeanor; in particular, we note their age, sex, skin color, features, dress, and whether they speak our language with our accent. Subconscious influences may also be at work - such as the resemblance a person may have to other individuals we have known - in which case we tend to ascribe to our new acquaintance some of the same characteristics we associate with the former. This is one more example of how our minds define a new concept - in this case of a person - in terms of categories or concepts with which we are already familiar. We rely heavily on our first impressions since placing an unjustified trust in a new acquaintance may be dangerous, and immediate action may be required.

In fact, so powerful is the imperative to dissociate oneself and one's family, from those who are untrustworthy, that it evokes one of the most intense emotions to which humans are subject - anger. This emotion is particularly strongly aroused by even the hint of disloyalty - the thought that one in whom an individual, or the members of the tribe placed their trust has betrayed them. Such a person is viewed as an immediate danger to the members, their offspring and the tribe, as a result of which the members feel a compulsion to rid the tribe of the offender instantly - sometimes by violent means - upon discovering the betrayal.

We see this frequently in modern society where people are drummed out of the service, banished, excommunicated, expelled from clubs, schools, religious and military organizations, nations, etc., usually in disgrace for unbecoming behavior, for treachery, or for disloyalty. We see this as well in the reaction of the members of society towards criminals, who they feel have violated the trust society has afforded all its citizens, and whom, therefore, must be isolated (imprisoned), or even executed. We also see this in individuals who suffer, or imagine they suffer, a slight or betrayal by another individual or group. The usual reaction is indignation - or anger - depending on the magnitude of the injury and the degree of the trust that has been violated as perceived by the individual.

But Isn't Skepticism Rational?

While our reactions to treachery may be emotional, it could be argued that skepticism is, nevertheless, basically rational, and that we judge people simply because we think it to be in our best interests to do so. I would agree that skepticism has a large mental component, requiring judgment, but still insist that the motivation to employ a skeptical attitude is basically an emotional inherent urge, one that at times we feel difficult to resist. We have seen its importance to our survival, and once again I insist that a more consistent application of this important function will result if it takes the form of a persistent urge rather than a requirement that we make a rational decision to do so. People show a wide variation in the degree to which they are either 'skeptical' or 'tolerant', and to my knowledge there is no evidence that this variation is in any way correlated with intelligence. In fact, many of us are acquainted with those whom we consider to be intelligent, but nevertheless 'stubbornly biased' (a trait that we seldom apply to ourselves!) Thus, according to my definition - the *urge* to be skeptical, since it is not strictly intellectual, must be emotional, while the *act of being skeptical*, is intellectual.

The Joys of Cynicism

In support of the contention that one of the goals set by our genes is for us to exercise our skeptical faculties, consider the obvious pleasure we derive from our cynical attitudes. We exhibit this through our enjoyment of political cartoons and jokes. We are titillated by the discovery of peccadilloes amongst the famous and find humor in tales that reveal hypocritical statements or attitudes held by people, particularly those not in our group, such as politicians and others in authority. Many of us have been witness to raconteurs who, after relating a speech given with an air of honesty by someone of importance, then state with obvious relish: "But he lied through his teeth!"

This pleasure is generated by exercising our ability to detect dishonesty, particularly in those occupying positions of trust (a group to which we ourselves do not belong). We exercise our skeptical attributes simply because doing so gives us pleasure, and - as we have seen - the reason it does so, is that it promotes an activity which in the past has contributed to our survival as a species.

It Pays Not To Be Excessive

As with altruism and egoism, skepticism cannot be too intense, since a group of highly skeptical individuals would disintegrate with no member trusting any other. On the other hand, skepticism, like altruism and egoism, is complex and is therefore likely to be polygenetic, and to be expressed with a different intensity in each individual.

Thus, selective pressures will have tended to optimize the balance of these three traits, and in this way will have guaranteed the success of the society in which we all live today. Thus modern society, which we may define as a homogeneous symbiosis, must have been initiated by the banding together of a number of individuals who felt that they could trust each other. Each member of these early bands or tribes would have been in constant judgment on the others and any members who raised doubts in the minds of their fellows as to their sincerity, or loyalty to the group, would have been considered to be undesirable and killed, or they and their family excluded from the group. In fact all individuals who lied, cheated, stole from other members, refused to participate in hunting or fighting or were generally perceived as being unreliable would have been expelled from the tribe and, as a result, they and their families would have become vulnerable and their gene line extinct.

Those possessing an intense altruistic trait, on the other hand, would have been of considerable benefit to the tribe and therefore given a preferred status. They would not have increased in numbers within the tribe, however, since, in its most extreme form, this trait would be detrimental to its possessor, who would be driven to self-neglect by a passion to serve the tribal society. Such individuals not only suffer physically, but tend to deny themselves the indulgence of sexual reproduction, further reducing the occurrence of genes for altruism. On the other hand, these genes would not be entirely eliminated from the tribal gene pool, since they, when expressed to a lesser degree, give rise to the trait of trustworthiness.

Nor would the cheater genes be entirely eliminated from the gene pool of a successful society, due to the biological variability of the essential egoistic trait and the fact that skepticism - the cheater's nemesis - could, if too intense, destroy a group. In fact, the cheaters, in their defense, would tend to have developed a trait called 'duplicity' or 'cunning' - the ability to deceive the skeptics.

EVOLUTION OF SOCIETY

The Optimum Is a Balance of Egoism, Altruism and Skepticism.

We see, then, that there are four characteristics or urges that the genes must confer on the individuals who are carrying them to ensure their own perpetuation. First they must compel their carriers to be concerned with their own immediate welfare, and we classify the actions motivated by this concern (or emotion) as **egoistic** or **selfish**. Second, they should instill in their carriers **gregariousness** - a powerful emotional drive to belong to a group or tribe for their own and their families' protection, and an intense dread of rejection by the tribe. This characteristic, in turn, leads the individual to find and join a group of other individuals who, they believe, will act in their best interests, and in particular, those of their offspring. In accomplishing this, however, they must avoid associating with cheaters by exercising the third trait provided by the genes - skepticism. At the same time, they must overcome the skepticism of others who are also attempting to form beneficial associations, by appearing to be reliable themselves. This requires that they convince the other members of the tribe that they are prepared to reciprocate by showing genuine compassion and concern for the others' welfare, and to do this, in turn, it is necessary that they possess, at least to some degree, the fourth characteristic provided by the genes - **altruism**. Without skepticism, however, altruism is unworkable.

Again I would stress that to guarantee that our acts are made in our own best interests (and those of our genes) by ensuring that we become members of a suitable society - these qualities must be inherent, which is to say that the urge to perform these acts should be genetically specified in each of us. This is particularly important in the case of altruism, since if we are not inherently or genuinely concerned with the welfare of the other members, but are simply attempting to gain the advantages of association, we will have to ingratiate ourselves to the group by assuming the constant pretense of reliability. Such dissemblance is dangerous, however, since a single mistake can have drastic results and therefore we will be forced to maintain perpetual vigilance of our own actions. This danger can be avoided, however, if we have at least some *genuine*, inherent concern for others and a desire to act accordingly; in other words we must feel 'good' about doing so. At the same time, there must be within us a negative emotional compulsion against performing acts that are 'bad' or harmful to the group. This takes the form of **guilt**, an *emotion, which punishes us for deeds contrary to our concept of good and to which we refer as our* **conscience**.

It Pays To Be Good...

Thus it has evolved that altruistic actions have a positive connotation in our minds, which is why they are associated with such concepts as 'good', 'noble', 'honorable', etc., while the actions of self-serving individuals are ' base' and 'despicable'. These are preconceptions that we inherit and that appear to us for this reason to be very real. We find it hard to believe that 'goodness' is not an absolute quality and that there are not universal rules of good behavior. In fact, so powerful are the concepts good and its converse **evil** that they assume palpable, even concrete, shapes in our subconscious minds to which some of us ascribe such anthropomorphic terms as 'angels' and **'devils'**. The intensity with which we hold these beliefs is not surprising since there would be no selective advantage to us in questioning them.

We see then that an inherent tendency toward moral behavior has indeed been selected in most individuals.

...but Not Too Good!

Because goodness is a preconception that most of us have, we are led to believe in the absolute of perfection. We visualize the perfect person as possessing infinite goodness and it is against this standard that we find ourselves wanting. In fact, it is this deficit that has given rise to the concept of **original sin**.

Few, if any, individuals attain perfection, however, since such intense goodness, or altruism, would be destructive to that individual. Thus, once again, we see that the function of natural selection is to *optimize*, but not necessarily to *maximize*! Thus it is that by operating at this functional optimum we find ourselves to be good - *but not perfect!*

Why We Want To Be Good

But while the concept of 'good' is essentially emotional, it also has a rational component. We all agree that for society to operate effectively, all members should not only obey the rules, but should convince others,

EVOLUTION OF SOCIETY

particularly their own offspring, to do so as well. This gives us a rationale for our own actions in seeking the emotional goal of attaining security.

There is also another rationale for acting in a morally responsible manner towards others - our desire to gain status within the group, or to be 'well thought of' by the other members. This is, of course, driven by our own egoism and need for self-respect.

In summary, then, there are three main reasons why we perform 'good' acts. First, there is the strictly emotional requirement stemming from our gregariousness, our need for security or fear of rejection by the group, and our desire for the approbation of others (our need to be liked), as demanded by our egos.

Second, there is the more cerebral conviction that most of us hold, which is that a sound union requires the cooperation of all, and we reason that - as our contribution to the public good - we should ourselves act in a morally acceptable manner.

Finally, there is the purely emotional feeling that 'good' deeds generate in us - a feeling of elation when assisting others, and a feeling of guilt or remorse for wrongs we have done to others - which leads to altruism. (A deed can only be truly altruistic, however, if our urge to perform it is independent of whether others are, or may become, aware of it.)

The most important reason for possessing genuine goodness is that it makes us acceptable to others, and it is for this reason that being good gives us pleasure. Most humans are basically kind and considerate of others and find enjoyment in performing simple acts of courtesy, such as holding a door open, or greeting others with evident pleasure. I believe this to be inherent (rather than learned) since it is quite common to observe children showing disapproval of acts performed by a parent that they feel, are unethical. This we observe, even though it is the parents who are expected to teach the children ethical living - both by instruction and example!

The Communal or Group Concept

We have already seen that we are born with an important basic concept - the 'self' - that leads to the trait called 'egoism'. On the other hand, we are also gregarious and have a strong desire to belong to a group. I suggest, therefore, that another concept we are born with - the **group** or **communal concept** - acts as *a focal point to which our gregarious urge directs our loyalty*. As with most preconceptions, it initially lies dormant, awaiting definition (or imprintation). In our early years, the 'group' is defined as consisting of our immediate family and those persons around us whom our parents and friends approve of - in short, those who are most likely to belong to our own gene pool. Others whom we meet in later life having similar appearance and manners are also accepted as belonging to our group, while those who have different features or dress, or who act or speak differently, are not accepted as 'one of us' (nor are they likely to belong to our immediate gene pool) and are therefore treated at best with reserve.

As with all preconcepts, the group concept has two important characteristics. First it is personal - initially being vague and requiring definition by rational processes based on observation and experience (i. e. we must be imprinted with our society's concept of who are acceptable members). It therefore takes a different form in each individual, depending on both the heredity and the personal experiences of that individual. With some, its intensity gives rise to fervent **religious beliefs**, causing them to commit to specific sects, while in others, it takes the form of **nationalism** or adherence to a political party, philosophy or movement. In still others it is the **gang** or brotherhood, which demands their absolute fealty. In all cases, however, it has a positive connotation, and in return for the demands the group makes on the individual, it provides feelings of security and becomes a sanctuary.

Second, for it to be effective, its reality in the mind of the individual must be unquestioned and her or his acceptance of its authority, unshakable. Again it must be pointed out that for it to fulfill its function of promoting the gene line, the individual must accept it - absolutely. In some individuals this leads to an inflexible, arrogant, self-assured conviction in the righteousness of their beliefs, and a hostile or violent reaction toward those who would question these beliefs or attempt to dissuade adherents from practicing their rituals, since to deny the group in any way, could result in their banishment - a frightening prospect. It is these attitudes that form the basis of religious and nationalistic conservatism.

To many it is the central theme of their lives and they are prepared to sacrifice anything, including in some cases their own lives, to promote the welfare of that which they perceive to be the group. Although it is not always well defined, it inspires in us the feeling that there is 'a power greater' than ourselves, which transcends our mundane associations and demands our allegiance; that inspires us with 'awe' and to which many of us give the name **God** or **the nation**. Like all our preconceptions we are convinced that it is absolute and exists 'in essence' outside our minds and even though we may be unclear as to its true nature, we are, nevertheless, convinced that: "There must be something out there."

This desire, this urge, this need to believe or have faith in a **superior power**, is, of course, emotional rather than rational, but so powerful is it that, for many, the existence of God is taken to be an established fact and rationalization is frequently employed to justify it. Thus religious apologists, who define **God** as being *omniscient, omnipotent and the author of all things*, claim to be able to prove Her or His existence logically, ignoring the fact that to do so requires that She or He be subject to the 'laws of logic' - of which She or He is presumably the author! But if this were the case, these laws would transcend God Who created them - a logical inconsistency. We are, in fact, being asked to view God as a great spider, who, having spun Its web of logic, is now trapped in it! Such a view leads many to accept the **agnostic's** position - that *due to God's nature (or should we say, the way in which She or He is defined?), Her or His existence can be neither proven nor disproven.*

The Origin of Religions

In an attempt to satisfy our need to belong, we seek association with a group, usually consisting initially, as we have noted, of those with whom we are familiar, such as our family and their immediate acquaintances, most of who are of our own race and culture, and with whom we have a comfortable rapport. As our group increases in size, its continued cohesion will demand that there be a focus - an embodiment of our concept of the group - to which our reverence may be directed, so that a group definition of God must be found. The more reverent members, (those having the most intense communal concept) called variously shamans, priests, prophets, etc., will advance such a definition, which will become an important part of the **persistent wisdom** of the group and form the basis of a religion. We are, through teaching, exposed to this concept of God, Whom we generally acknowledge in order to be accepted by the group, because of our need of a focus for our veneration and because we feel that if many people believe it, it must be true. This is in fact another expression of our desire to conform, to be a member of the herd and the more closely we conform to the tribal ideal of the **'good' member**, the greater the respect we command and the more secure we feel.

Most religions also appeal strongly to the ego by promoting the idea that the material world - whose power over us we contemplate with dread - actually exists for our benefit and that we, as part of a grand plan whose vistas reach far beyond the material universe, are ultimately superior to it. We refuse to accept any restriction in a temporal sense and deny the undeniable fact of death by insisting that we, in essence, endure to eternity. Such a belief also alleviates the shock we feel when confronted with the death of one upon whom we have depended - and who may have occupied the very kernel of our lives - by allowing us to perceive such a loss as temporary.

Again we should point out that the **successful gene** is *one that makes us experience pleasure in pursuing the urges it instills*. Thus we have a desire to submit to the concept of God or the nation with which we have been imprinted and furthermore we not only *believe* in God and the nation, but *want* to believe in them!

Anthropomorphism

Because of the importance that membership in a suitable society has for our species and the genes we carry, it is imperative that humans manifest an ability to join and to function adequately in a group. Thus - as we have seen - there will have been a selection of those individuals whose behavioral characteristics are such as - not only to promote their membership in a group - but to enhance their status amongst their cohorts as well.

As already noted, a sincere concern for our fellow members and the capability of detecting insincerity in others, are basic requirements in this regard. But in addition we must have the ability to assess the effects which our behavior is having on the other members of our group since we need to make judgments as to how we ourselves should act to enhance the esteem with which they regard us, and, in addition, to convince them to behave in ways which we feel are to our advantage.

Perhaps the most obvious means by which we communicate our feelings is through facial expressions, such as, for example, those of joy and anger. The ability to recognize the facial features of others, and to assess their moods, are themselves inherent qualities which most of us possess - again since they promote our social skills and welfare.

There is, however, another important means by which we may estimate the reaction others are having - or may have - to actions we ourselves perform, which we may term **personification**. This is an urge to regard others as having the same feelings as we ourselves might have toward any given circumstance. In other words, we have *an inherent tendency to project our feelings and desires on others.* While this process is unlikely to be accurate, it is at least approximate, and one of the few methods open to us in making estimates of the feelings of others. It is therefore very important to our welfare, and it is for this reason that an *urge* to personify will have been introduced as a goal early in our evolution toward a communal species.

In fact, so powerful is this urge, that we tend to project our feelings - not only on other persons - but on other animals and even inanimate objects and forces of nature as well. We see this frequently in ancient mythology, in which gods of human form are assigned mastery over many of these objects and forces. We see this also in modern mythology that **anthropomorphizes** everything from Mickey Mouse to God!

Thus it is that we personify the communal belief we all have that there is a force greater than ourselves, by naming that force **God**, and by imbuing Him with all the human emotions, not only of love and mercy, but of jealousy and vengefulness as well!

None of us is immune; even those who claim to be scientists and boast of objectiveness, frequently lapse into the use of personification and speak of the **purpose** associated with the functioning of natural selection. Natural selection, however, is a mindless process that has *no purpose - only function!*

Taboos and Rituals

The cohesiveness of a group can be enhanced by contrasting it with other groups, so it is in the interest of the group to increase this contrast by enforcing a uniformity on its members. This leads to standards of dress, speech, and customs (including taboos) within the group, and with the studied avoidance, and even derision, of the dress, speech, and customs of rival groups. Religion also serves to promote the cohesion and welfare of the group with which it is closely associated. The **good member** is therefore one who submits to religious authority by accepting the definition of God unquestioningly and by paying homage to Her or Him (as a personification of the group authority) through the performance of rituals. These also serve to define the group and to distinguish it from other groups or tribes who do not perform the same rituals - or to put it more simply - to separate 'us' from 'them'.

In addition, the periodic performance of these rituals by the members reaffirms their submission to the group authority. This is demanded by tradition since the needs of the self frequently conflict with those of the group. We, for our part, attempt to convince our skeptical comrades of our own trustworthiness, and show our devotion and loyalty to the group by cooperating in the performance of the rituals. These performances must be seen by the others whom we wish to impress and are therefore usually performed in public and preferably in concert. The essential aspect of the ritual is to demonstrate our submission to the **greater good** as personified by God or the national flag or banner. Rituals usually consist of exposing oneself to the mercy of the powerful entity by bearing one's head or assuming a vulnerable position - bowing, kneeling, or even prostrating oneself before an idol or flag or other symbol of the group entity. St. Augustine's conundrum as to why

> ...when men pray, they do with the members of their bodies what befits suppliants - when they bend their knees and stretch out their hands, or even prostrate themselves . . . . although their invisible will and the intention of their heart is known to God.

is simply explained by an inherent need to convince our skeptical associates of our own sincerity. Since such an act serves to strengthen our standing in the group, it is in our best interests and therefore has a positive connotation, making us feel 'good, loyal and devout'. On the other hand, if we fail the group by not performing the rituals demanded of it by tradition, we feel uncomfortable and guilty or disloyal.

Feelings of guilt are frequently exploited by religion to promote moral behavior and loyalty in its adherents. This is particularly true of the Christian religion, which likens each transgression to driving a nail into the very flesh of the Son of God! Perhaps such vivid imagery explains the ability of the Christian church to have survived for so long.

God Sees All and Knows All

As we have pointed out, any attempt to cheat by members of a group raises the danger of discovery, which can have dire results. The revelation that an individual has taken more than her or his fair share of food from the tribal supplies, for example, would have resulted in death or banishment for the offender and family. To lessen the probability of making such a mistake, therefore, most fit individuals possess an inherent feeling that their actions are constantly under scrutiny. This feeling bestows an important survival advantage on its possessor, and it is for this reason that many of us possess it. It also gives rise to the conviction that an omniscient God is aware, not only of our acts but of our thoughts as well, or to quote St. Augustine again: "(men's) invisible will and the intention of their heart is known to God." In fact, so thoroughly convinced are the devout of the absolute, highly pervasive nature of God that they continue to perform their rituals even in private.

But What is Goodness?

We define humans as moral animals, by which we imply that they show genuine concern for the welfare of the society of which they are members - as well as for other members of that society. This is an emotional characteristic in the sense in which it was defined above, since it influences us to act in ways that make us acceptable to other members of society. Furthermore, we define a 'good' person as one who loves his fellow man, and we measure this degree of 'goodness' by assessing a person's concern for the welfare of others relative to that of her or his own.

If we could make a quantitative measure of 'goodness' as the ratio of the intensity of altruism to egoism and plot it as the intensity factor in a population distribution curve, we would likely find that it ranged from zero for the totally self-centered to a very high figure for the highly altruistic. Since the former would have been rejected by earlier skeptical societies and the latter suffer from self-neglect, both extreme positions would be dangerous for any individuals occupying them, and would therefore have a very low population density. The intensity factor for the remaining members of the species, however, should show the usual biological variance, and when plotted, form a distribution curve whose peak - determined by natural selection - is that providing the greatest contribution to the survival of the individual.

We frequently refer to some persons as 'spiritual' by which we may imply 'moral' and 'devout' as defined above. This definition is vague, however, since it invokes the mystical essence of the **spirit**. We may also insist that for persons to be moral they must have 'faith', or believe in another mystical essence, 'God'. But again we are simply implying that the person who believes in, or submits to God, is one who accepts the supremacy of the commune, placing its welfare above that of her or his own.

Evil is defined as that which is potentially harmful to us and our group and we consider it, in its extreme form (along with 'good'), to be absolute. In reality, it is simply a personification of those concepts which have inimical connotations and which are therefore frightening to us.

The Origins of Conservatism...

One of the most important advantages that individuals gain from group membership is to share in the **persistent wisdom** of the tribe - *the knowledge that the tribe has accumulated through experience.* By accepting the *modus vivendi* of the older members of the tribe, the younger members can avoid the mistakes that their predecessors have made. They can, in fact, assume that the manner in which the tribal members live, while perhaps not the most efficacious, is at least safe and therefore should be emulated. In fact there is a decided risk in ignoring the tribal customs, such as avoiding foods that in the past have proved to be harmful. Thus, the gene complement that imbues its carrier with a desire to accept and copy the customs adopted by the tribe will provide a survival advantage to those who possess it over those who do not and will therefore become established in the population. This desire, which results in the characteristic of human personality we term **conservatism**, is an urge that at times can overwhelm our rational processes, and therefore should be classified as an emotion, according to the definition of the latter given above.

In an attempt to distance their tribe from others, tribal members frequently establish taboos, such as dietary proscriptions, which demand that they view certain foods as unsuitable - mainly because of their hatred for rivals who consume them. Initially certain practices may be adopted in an attempt to protect society from a real or imagined danger, but, once established, their practice may continue in the form of a taboo, even after the threat has vanished. Taboos also arise from an inherent aversion to certain acts, such as homosexuality or incest, which, because of their detrimental effect on reproduction, the majority of members find inherently repugnant.

Once any ritual or taboo becomes established in a society, its preservation is ensured by the desire of the members to conform - which they do by continuing its practice - and because of the guilt they would otherwise feel in abandoning it. It is also sustained by the conservative element within the tribe and by the fact that such practices serve to define the tribe. Perhaps this attitude explains the irrational belief in **the wisdom of the ages**, which promotes the conviction that our ancestors were inevitably: "much wiser than we", or that they possessed secret or 'revealed knowledge' and that therefore we should not deny their teachings or the authority of their holy scriptures.

This belief, together with a loyalty to the creeds instilled during youth, are essentially emotional and demand to be supported by the intellect that they dominate. Thus are generated religious dogmas and such other rationalizations as that of creationism. Furthermore, those harboring such beliefs frequently develop a fear of the consequences of being dissuaded from their acceptance. The fact is, however, that such individuals are duped by their genes into the belief that it is their intellect, rather than their emotions, that presents them with 'reality' or 'The Truth'.

...and Dissension

Again, as with other qualities, conservatism can be harmful in excess. It can, for example, inhibit the ability of the individual or the tribe to adapt to changing conditions through the alteration or even rejection of established customs when changing conditions render them less helpful or even harmful.

We have seen that curiosity, an emotional requirement to examine and explore alternatives, is also an important aspect of human nature. However the knowledge gained by experimenting is useless if conservatism prevents its application where appropriate. At such times, a nonconformist, **liberal** or **innovative** urge - a desire for change - is advantageous, but again, only if active at moderate strength. Once more we see that a balance of two opposing desires works to the advantage of both the individual and the society of which she or he is a member and once more I would emphasize that the optimum balance operating in present day societies, has been achieved by selective forces. The presence of both emotions, or urges, in each individual, however, requires that the conflicting actions demanded by each desire be adjudicated - a function performed by the intellect.

The Importance of the Communal Concept

So we see that the possession of the communal concept modifies our behavior profoundly, causing us to form the tribes, societies, or nations so important to our survival. It also gives rise to concepts such as 'good' and 'noble' and to their converse. Any action that promotes the individual at the expense of the group is '**selfish**' and thus 'despicable'. To kill a member of one's own group is a crime and a sin, whereas to kill an 'enemy' makes one a 'hero' and to refuse to do so, makes one a 'coward'. To violate the strictures that the group imposes on our activities, results in the genuine pain of 'guilt'. Furthermore, we reject others who act ignobly and such rejection, or excommunication, can be frightening for the one rejected, since not to be a member of a group leaves one vulnerable. Thus, we constantly seek the approbation and 'respect' of the group.

The Structure of Groups

The structure of groups varies according to their history - groups under pressure tending to be more highly structured and to impose a greater discipline on their members. Almost all groups possess a hierarchy, with usually dominant males at the highest level of authority. From these a leader arises whose power depends on the rigidity of the group. In the larger, more tightly controlled groups, where the leader is more aloof, he may be revered and come to personify the group concept - that is, to exercise divine rights and ultimately, to be deified.

In less structured groups, or groups in which communications are more advanced (such as some of our modern societies), the leader is more accessible, and therefore more familiar to the average members, who, being privy to the leader's failings, find it harder to associate him with the nobler aspects of the communal concept. This concept carries with it the emotional requirement that the members revere it and submit to its authority, and as they must have a focus for their veneration, feel there must be an entity that transcends human failings and it is to this they give the name **God** or **nation**.

The Extent of Our Moral Obligations - the Moral Domain

The initial group was, of course, the tribe, which consisted mostly of individuals who shared many of their genes in common and it was therefore natural that the welfare of the tribe to which an individual belonged should take precedence over other tribes or their members. Since there was frequent competition between various tribes and groups for land and resources, there would always have been the need for individuals at times to be ruthless towards those who were not members of their own tribe in the interest of those who were. Thus while they felt a strong need to treat their own fellow members according to the moral standards of their tribe, these standards did not apply in their relationship with other persons.

This **moral dichotomy** meant that they had to distinguish between those individuals to whom the **moral imperative** applied - those within their **moral domain**, or **compass** - and those to whom it did not - that is, those whose trust and respect they desired and those to whom they felt indifference, contempt or even 'hatred'. To promote this distinction, humans possess another preconception, the **out-group**, or in short, 'them' as opposed to the **in-group** or 'us'. In the next chapter, we shall consider the importance of these concepts in the rapid evolution of modern humans.

Although we generally treat members of other societies whom we have just met with cautious respect, we are all too prone to heed those who would raise our ire against another group by claiming that they pose a threat to us. Since they are not one of us, it is easy to suspend any moral obligations we might initially have felt towards them. The least of our reactions to them is indifference, but as the perceived provocation increases, our feelings against them grow in intensity, and they become the hated **enemy** who may, or even *must* be driven away or destroyed. The important point is that *we feel morally obliged to treat only those who are members of our in-group with consideration and respect.* Relegating a person or group to the category of 'enemy' relieves us of any restraint in our dealings with them - ***the moral imperative does not apply to an 'enemy'.*** It is therefore very important how we form our concept of 'the group', remembering that since the group is an emotional preconception, it must be defined and this definition comes from experience, particularly from the teaching and behavioral examples of those whom we respect most.

The Result Is a Balance of the 'Self' and the 'Group' Concepts

The demands of the 'self' and the 'group' shape our behavior. Frequently they clash, requiring a rational, or more often an emotional resolution as to what action we should take. As with most biological systems, there is a statistical variation in the importance that each of these concepts has in determining an individual's behavior. With some, a weak communal concept coupled with a strong egoism results in an antisocial or even totally amoral attitude, threatening the integrity of the group.

On the other hand, a weak self-concept can result in fervent self-denial, which, as we have seen, can destroy an individual and while on occasion, self-sacrifice can be an advantage to the group, wholesale activity of this kind among the population of a society will eventually destroy it. An excessive in-group/out-group concept leads to nationalism, racism, or religious fervor, which might have been important to the survival of the earlier tribes, but is perhaps less important in today's pluralistic societies. Obviously, a balance in the effect of these drives within a social group is required and - as with egoism, altruism, and skepticism - natural selection has provided such a balance between the intensity factors for egoism and group loyalty. Thus, while within our present society there are individuals tending to favor one or other extreme, the interests of the vast majority lie somewhere in between, and on average, the influence of each concept or urge is such as to ensure the formation of viable groups while simultaneously promoting the survival of the individual.

And In Conclusion...

Among the claims made in this chapter, the least controversial is probably the one in which I state that most of us possess a skeptical sense. After all, you, the reader, have no doubt viewed these few pages through critical eyes; if you haven't, I congratulate you on your ability to suppress your boredom sufficiently to have progressed this far in my thesis!

My claim that skepticism is necessary to make altruism function in society will perhaps be questioned by some. However, the greatest wave of dissension will, no doubt, rise against my classification of the 'urge to be skeptical' as an emotion with which our genes endow us because it has ensured their - and our - past success. Our egos demand that we view ourselves as basically intelligent beings, whose opinions are shaped by the gentle currents of the intellect - and not by the violent storms of emotion! However, I would remind those who believe detached, unemotional thought to be possible, that most of us possess a very powerful and very human characteristic: *we hate to be wrong*, and will go to almost any lengths to prove that we were right all along, even in the face of overwhelming evidence to the contrary!

CHAPTER SEVEN

THE SOCIETY OF THE HUNTER-GATHERERS

In this and the next chapter, we will consider the evolution of modern societies - starting with the hunter-gatherers and attempting to show how modern European urbanized societies derived from them. Let us begin by considering a typical example of a hunter-gather society - that of the northern North American natives.

The Journals of Samuel Hearne
In 1715 the Hudson's Bay Company established a trading post at Fort Prince of Wales on the shores of Hudson's Bay, the purpose of which was to trade with the natives indigenous to the area. Several of the natives attracted to this post brought samples of copper ore with them. When asked about the origin of the copper they reported that the source was near the mouth of a large river. It was assumed by the company personnel to be a river emptying into Hudson's Bay, but efforts to locate it by water failed.

In 1769 Samuel Hearne was commissioned by the company to make a search for the river and its mineral deposits in the inland area west of the fort. His first two attempts failed due to a lack of reliable guidance. On his third attempt, however, he enlisted the services of a highly competent Northern Indian guide named Matonabbee, who made it possible for him to reach his goal. During these excursions - which lasted more than two and a half years - he was the only white man in the party and the only white man many of the natives he encountered had yet seen. Although Hearne kept extensive records of his life with the natives, these extremely valuable original journals appear to have been lost. Fortunately, however, a few copies are still extant and have been edited and published by the Champlain Society[1]; the extensive quotes that are reproduced below come directly from this publication. A somewhat abbreviated, but perhaps more readable version, edited by Farley Mowat, is also available[2].

The reason that Hearne's journals are so valuable is that they contain a recent account of the culture of the Northern Indians at a time when European influence on them had yet to become significant. These journals describe the customs and interrelationships of a people living in a basically nomadic hunter-gatherer society in what is now northern Canada, a rugged and unforgiving environment. Their culture, which likely originated in northern Asia tens of thousands of years before spreading to North America, was probably typical of the late Neolithic forerunners of most present-day northern hemisphere societies. It might be profitable in our present task, therefore, to consider the information these reports provide. Before doing so, however, perhaps we should assess their author, so as to estimate possible biases on his part.

Samuel Hearne

Samuel Hearne was born in London in 1745. After only three years of formal schooling, he enlisted in the Royal Navy at the age of eleven as servant to Viscount Hood with whom he saw much action throughout the Seven Years War. In 1766 he joined the Hudson's Bay Company, and was sent to Fort Prince of Wales, a trading post on the west coast of Hudson's Bay at the mouth of the Churchill River. It was from here that he made the excursions into the vast interior areas of land, which, until then, had been totally unknown to European culture.

Following these adventures, he helped to establish Cumberland House (in what is now southern Saskatchewan), the first major Hudson's Bay Company inland trading post and the one that probably saved the Company from financial disaster, threatened as it was at the time by competition from French and independent traders. In 1776 Hearne became governor of Fort Prince of Wales. Six years later, under treaties that the French had signed with the American rebel colonies, a French force attacked the fort. On observing that the size of the attacking forces was ten times that of his own, Hearne refused to sacrifice lives needlessly in a futile attempt to resist, and surrendered the fort. He was taken prisoner but later released and returned to England, where he was branded a coward by many. The explanation of his actions must have been acceptable to the Company, however, since immediately after peace was declared, he was sent back to restore the Fort.

Samuel Hearne was a kind, sensitive man who hated violence and suffering. His courage had been tested through seven years of war and twenty years in the North American wilderness, much of the time on his own amongst natives who obviously liked and respected him. His journals, written in an engaging style, show him to be an observant reporter.

The Land and Culture of the Chipewyans

The region occupied by the people to whom he refers as the "Northern Indians" (probably members of the now extinct Chipewyan nation) stretched for more than a thousand kilometers to the west of Hudson's Bay and included the northern part of the arboreal forests and the open tundra of the barren lands reaching to the Arctic Ocean. These people depended for their welfare almost entirely on the caribou, which, until that time, had been plentiful. The Indians stayed close to these animals who spent the winters south of the tree line (the northern boundary of forest growth) and migrated north into the barren lands in the summer. From the trees the Indians obtained birch bark and staves to make canoes, snowshoes and supports for their skin tents, while depending on the caribou for food and clothing.

The natives were able to kill large numbers of caribou at a time by driving them into 'pounds' - compounds constructed beforehand from trees and bushes - where they could be readily snared and slaughtered. Concerning the number of caribou (which he called deer) killed by the Indians, Hearne wrote:

> The great destruction which is made of the deer in those parts ....is almost incredible; and as they are never known to have more than one young at a time, it is wonderful that they do not become scarce; but so far is this from being the case, that the oldest Northern Indian in all their tribe will affirm that the deer are as plentiful now as they ever have been.
>
> It requires the prime parts of the skins of from eight to ten deer to make a complete suit of warm clothing for a grown person during the Winter; all of which should, if possible, be killed in the month of August, or early September; for after that time the hair is too long, and at the same time so loose in the pelt, that it will drop off at the slightest injury.
>
> Besides these skins, which must be in their hair, each person requires several others to be dressed into leather, for stockings and shoes, and light Summer clothing; several more are wanted in a parchment state, to make thongs for netting for their snowshoes, snares for deer, thongs for their sledges, and, in fact, for every other use where strings or lines of any kind are required; so that each person, on an average, expends in the course of a year, upward of twenty deerskins for clothing and domestic uses, exclusive of tent cloths, bags, and many other things which it is impossible to remember, and unnecessary to enumerate.

This observation is important since it shows that the hunter-gather lifestyle requires large numbers of animals to sustain it, and these in turn, must be supported by tracts of open land, which, especially in the northern climate, must be extensive.

It is not known how long this area has been occupied. It is possible that these natives settled here on originally coming to North America some ten to fifteen thousand years ago. On the other hand, they could have drifted north more recently from a more densely populated area to the south. They spoke a different language to that of the Cree, their southern neighbors, however, which would indicate a fairly lengthy isolation from them. It appears, therefore, that they had reached a stable population density in which their birth rate just balanced the loss by death and migration. This is supported by Hearne's observation that a relatively lengthy three-year period seemed to separate the successive pregnancies most Indian women experienced.

A Male Dominated Society

Their society, like many human societies, was heavily male-dominated. While recruiting Matonabbee as guide for his third expedition, Hearne quotes him as attributing the failure of the first two expeditions partly to the misconduct of the previous guides but mainly to the fact that no women accompanied them

> 'For,' said he, 'when all the men are heavy laden, they can neither hunt nor travel to any considerable distance; and in case they should meet with success in hunting, who is to carry the produce of their labor?' 'Women' added he 'were made for labor; one of them can carry or haul as much as two men can do. They also pitch our tents, make and mend our clothing, keep us warm at night; and, in fact there is no such thing as traveling any considerable distance, or for any length of time, in this country, without their assistance.' 'Woman,' said he again, 'though they do every thing, are maintained at a trifling expense; for as they always stand and cook, the very licking of their fingers in scarce times is sufficient for their subsistence.

Hearne notes that at one point

> Matonabbee purchased another wife (from some Northern Indians); so that he now had no less than seven, most of whom, for size would have made good grenadiers. He prided himself much in the height and strength of his wives, and would frequently say, few women would carry or haul heavier loads; and though they had, in general, a very masculine appearance, he preferred them to those of a more delicate form and moderate stature. In a country like this, where a partner in excessive hard labor is the chief motive for the union, and where the softer endearments of conjugal life are only considered as a secondary object, there seemed to be great propriety in such a choice.

As in many modern societies, wife-beating was a culturally acceptable practice, since, as Hearne observed,

> As to their (the women's) temper, it is of little consequence; for the men have a wonderful facility in making the most stubborn comply with as much alacrity as could possibly be expected ... knowing what is commanded must be done. They are, in fact, all kept at a great distance, and the rank they hold in the opinion of the men cannot be better expressed or explained, than by observing the method of treating or serving them at meals, which would appear very humiliating, to an European woman, though custom makes it sit light on those whose lot it is to bear it. It is necessary to observe, that when the men kill any large beast, the women are always sent to bring it to the tent: when it is brought there every operation it undergoes, such as splitting, drying, pounding, &c. is performed by women. When any thing is prepared for eating, it is the women who cook it; and when it is done, the wives and daughters of the greatest Captains in the country are never served, till all the males, even those who are in the capacity of servants, have eaten what they think proper; and in times of scarcity it is frequently their lot to be left without a single morsel.

Arranged marriages were as common in Indian society as in many other societies

> Their marriages are not attended with any ceremony; all matches are made by the parents, or next of kin. On those occasions the women seem to have no choice, but implicitly obey the will of their parents, who always endeavour to marry their daughters to those who seem most likely to be capable of maintaining them, let their age, person, or disposition (of these prospective husbands) be ever so despicable.
>
> The girls are always betrothed when children, but never to those of equal age, which is doubtless sound policy with people in their situation, where the existence of a family depends entirely on the abilities and industry of a single man. For this reason the girls are often disproportionately matched for age, that it is very common to see men of thirty-five or forty years have young girls of ten or twelve, and sometimes younger. From the early age of eight or nine years, they are prohibited by custom from joining in the most innocent amusements with children of the opposite sex; so that when sitting in their tents, or even when traveling, they are watched and guarded with an unremitting attention as cannot be exceeded by the most

rigid discipline of an English boarding-school. Custom, however, and constant example, make such uncommon restraint and confinement sit lightly on them.

This attitude toward marriage appears to be very similar to those of other male-dominated societies in which the father asserts a proprietary interest in his daughter's womb - presumably because his own genes are enshrined there. He therefore considers it his duty to guard this possession and to transfer its ownership only to another male deemed by him to be a worthy recipient. This attitude has reached its culmination in the Afro-Eurasian practice of female genital mutilation - euphemistically termed 'female circumcision' - still practiced by some present-day cultures. This procedure reduces the sexual pleasure the female experiences so as to diminish the danger that she might exercise her own propriety rights. In some cases the womb is partially closed by stitching, which effectively seals it against violation until the transfer of ownership has taken place.

Mates were also obtained in the Indian society by barter and by ritualized fighting, just as with many other species. Again, according to Hearne:

> It has ever been the custom among these people for the men to wrestle for any woman to whom they are attached; and, of course, the strongest party always carries off the prize. A weak man, unless he be a good hunter and well-beloved, is seldom permitted to keep a wife that a stronger man thinks is worth his notice; for at any time when the wives of those strong wrestlers are heavy-laden either with furrs or provisions, they make no scruple of tearing another man's wife from his bosom, and making her bear a part of his luggage. This custom prevails throughout all their tribes, and causes a great spirit of emulation among their youth, who are, upon all occasions from their childhood, trying their strength and skill in wrestling. This enables them to protect their property and particularly their wives from the hands of those powerful ravishers, some of whom make almost a livelihood by taking what they please from the weaker parties, without making any return.
>
> The way in which they tear the women and other property from one another, though it has the appearance of the greatest brutality, can scarcely be called fighting. I never knew any of them to receive the least hurt

in these rencontres; the whole business seems to consist of hauling each other about by the hair of the head; they are seldom known either to strike or kick one another. It is not uncommon for one of them to cut off his hair and grease his ears immediately before the contest begins. This is done privately; and it is sometimes truly laughable, to see one of the parties strutting about with an air of great importance, and calling out, "Where is he? Why does he not come out?" when the other will bolt out with a clean shorn head and greased ears, rush on his antagonist, seize him by the hair and, though perhaps a much weaker man, soon drag him to the ground, while the stronger is not able to lay hold on him.

On these wrestling occasions the standers-by never attempt to interfere in the contest; even one brother offers not to assist another, unless it be with advice, which, as it is always delivered openly on the field during the contest, may, in fact, be said to be equally favourable to both parties. It sometimes happens that one of the wrestlers is superior in strength to the other; and if a woman be the cause of the contest, the weaker is frequently unwilling to yield, notwithstanding he is greatly overpowered. When this happens to be the case, the relations and friends, or other bye-standers, will sometimes join to persuade the weaker combatant to give up the contest, lest, by continuing it, he should get bruised and hurt, without the least probability of being able to protect what he is contending for.

As to divorces, Hearne notes that

they are pretty common among the Northern Indians; sometimes for incontinency, but more frequently for want of what they deem the necessary accomplishments or for bad behavior. This ceremony, in either case, consists of neither more nor less than a good drubbing, and turning the woman out of doors; telling her to go to her paramour or relations, according to the nature of the crime.

Wife-beating, as we have noted, was obviously accepted by the native culture, but there is no evidence that it was any more frequent in the Indian culture than in other cultures in which it is banned, but continues to be practiced in a clandestine manner; or ignored by the authorities who consider it a quite natural family affair.

During childbirth, the woman was left on her own without assistance, as Hearne tells us:

When a Northern Indian woman is taken in labor, a small tent is erected for her, at such a distance from the other tents that her cries cannot easily be heard, and the other women and young girls are her constant visitants: no male, except children in arms, ever offers to approach her. It is a circumstance perhaps to be lamented, that these people never attempt to assist one another on those occasions, even in the most critical cases. This is in some measure owing to delicacy, but more probably to an opinion they entertain that nature is abundantly sufficient to perform every thing required, without any external help whatever. When I informed them of the assistance which European women derive from the skill and attention of our midwives, they treated it with the utmost contempt; ironically observing, that the many hump-backs, bandy-legs, and other deformities so frequent among the English, were undoubtedly owing to the great skill of the persons who assisted in bringing them into the world, and to the extraordinary care of their nurses afterwards.

Safeguarding the Young

In the previous chapter, it was stressed that one of the most important contributions to survival that a communal lifestyle provides is that the offspring of its cooperating members continue to receive the support of other members of the group following the death of one or both parents. That this was so in the native society is evidenced in Hearne's observation that

it is a very common custom amongst the men of this country to exchange a night's lodging with each other's wives. But this is so far from being considered an act which is criminal, that it is esteemed by them as one of the strongest ties of friendship between two families; and in case of the death of either man, the other considers himself bound to support the children of the deceased. Those people are so far from viewing this engagement as a mere ceremony, like most of our Christian god-fathers and god-mothers, who, notwithstanding their vows are made in the most solemn manner, and in the presence of both God and man, scarcely ever afterward remember what they have promised, that there is not an instance of a Northern Indian having once neglected the duty he is supposed to have taken on himself to perform. The Indians, for all their bad qualities, are remarkably humane and charitable to the widows and children of departed friends; and ... few widows or orphans are ever unprovided for among them.

Matonabbee

On December 7, 1770, Hearne set out on his third journey, which proved to be a success mainly due to the presence of Matonabbee, a native of considerable stature. Matonabbee was the son of a Chipweyan by a slave woman bought from the Cree by the governor of the fort. He was born about 1736. His father died while he was still young and, according to custom, he was adopted by the Governor, Richard Norton. Shortly afterward, Norton returned to England and Matonabbee went to live with his Northern Indian relatives. He returned to the Fort in 1752 where he worked for several years. Hearne's description of him follows:

> In the course of his long stay at and near the Fort, it is no wonder that he should have become perfect master of the Southern Indian language and made some progress in the English. It was during this period that he gained some knowledge of the Christian faith; and he always declared, that it was too deep and intricate for his comprehension.... He had so much natural good sense and liberality of sentiment, however, as not to think that he had a right to ridicule any particular sect on account of their religious opinion. On the contrary, he declared, that he held them all in equal esteem, but was determined, as he came into this world, so would he go out of it, without professing any religion at all. Notwithstanding his aversion from religion, I have met with few Christians who possessed more good moral qualities, or fewer bad ones.
>
> It is impossible for any man to have been more punctual in the performance of a promise than he was; his scrupulous adherence to truth and honesty would have done honour to the most enlightened and devout Christian, while his benevolence and universal humanity to all the human race, according to his abilities and manner of life, could not have been exceeded by the most illustrious personage now on record.
>
> In stature, Matonabbee was above the common size, being nearly six feet high; and, except that his neck was rather (though not much) too short, he was one of the finest and best proportioned men that I ever saw. In complexion, he was dark, like the other Northern Indians, but his face was not disfigured by that ridiculous custom of marking the cheeks with

three or four black lines. His features were regular and agreeable, yet so strongly marked and expressive, that they formed a complete index of his mind; which, as he never intended to deceive or dissemble, he never wished to conceal. In conversation he was easy, lively and agreeable, but exceedingly modest; and at table the nobleness and elegance of his manners might have been admired by the first personages in the world; for to the vivacity of a Frenchman, and the sincerity of an Englishman, he added the gravity and nobleness of a Turk; all so happily blended, as to render his company and conversation universally pleasing.

He was remarkably fond of Spanish wines, though he never drank to excess; and as he would not partake of spirituous liquors, however fine in quality or plainly mixed, he was always master of himself. As no man is exempt from frailties, it is natural to suppose that as a man he had his share; but the greatest with which I can charge him is jealousy, and that sometimes carried him beyond the bounds of humanity.

In his early youth he discovered talents equal to the greatest task that could possibly be expected from an Indian. Accordingly the Governor engaged him, when but a youth, as an Ambassador and Mediator between the Northern Indians and the Athapuscow Tribe who till then had always been at war with each other. In the course of this embassy Matonabbee not only discovered the most brilliant and solid parts, but shewed an extensive knowledge of every advantage that could arise to both nations from a total suppression of hostilities; and at times he displayed such instances of personal courage and magnanimity as are rarely to be found among persons of superior condition and rank.

Hearne then describes several incidences during which Matonabbee was forced to display his courage and diplomacy in dealing with the treacheries of the tribes he encountered, and concludes that

Notwithstanding all these discouragements and great dangers, Matonabbee persevered with courage and resolution to visit the Athapuscow Indians for several years successively; and at length, by a uniform display of his pacific disposition, and by rendering a long train of good offices to those Indians, in return for their treachery and perfidy, he was so happy as to be the sole instrument of not only bringing about a lasting peace, but also of establishing a trade and reciprocal interest between the two nations.

As further proof of the humanity often displayed by Matonabbee, Hearne recounts an incident in which a Coppermine Indian was left on one shore of a river after all his effects, and the rest of the party, had been ferried to the other side. No one but Matonabbee would return for him because of the strong winds. Matonabbee, however, stripped himself naked to be ready to swim in case the canoe capsized, and successfully completed the rescue.

From this description of Matonabbee it is obvious that he was a man who would have attained considerable stature in any society. He was an individual whom most would have termed 'noble' since he showed great altruism, subjecting himself to almost overwhelming personal danger in pursuit of the good of his own people. His one failing, however, was his egoism (a failing among many great men) which resulted in the death of one of his wives after a beating he gave her when she cast aspersions on his ability to support all seven of his mates.

The Expedition

Under the direction of Matonabbee, the expedition had little trouble in reaching the Coppermine River, which empties into the Arctic Ocean some fifteen hundred kilometers west and north of the Fort. The incidence that took place following their arrival is best related in Hearne's words:

> a great number of Indians entered into combination with those of my party to accompany us to the Copper-mine River; and with no other intent than to murder the Eskimaux, who are understood to frequent that river in considerable numbers. This scheme, notwithstanding the trouble and fatigue, as well as danger, with which it must be obviously attended, was nevertheless so universally approved by those people, that for some time almost every man who joined us proposed to be of the party.
>
> When I was acquainted with the intentions of my companions, and saw the warlike preparations that were carrying on, I endeavoured as much as possible to persuade them from putting their inhuman design into execution; but so far were my intreaties from having the wished-for effect, that it was concluded I was actuated by cowardice; and they told me, with great marks of derision, that I was afraid of the Eskimaux. As I knew that my personal safety depended in a great measure on the favourable opinion they entertained of me in this respect, I was obliged to change my tone, and replied that I did not care if they rendered the name and race of the

Eskimaux extinct; adding at the same time, that though I was no enemy to the Eskimaux, and did not see the necessity of attacking them without cause, yet if I should find it necessary to do it, for the protection of any one of my company, my own safety out of the question, so far from being afraid of a poor defenceless Eskimaux, whom I despised more than feared, nothing should be wanting on my part to protect all who were with me. This declaration was received with great satisfaction; and I never afterwards ventured to interfere with any of their war plans.

The Massacre.

Soon after their arrival at the Coppermine river, three Indians were sent off as spies in order to see if any Eskimos were inhabiting the river-side between the raiders and the sea. On their return they reported that there were five tents of Eskimos camped about twelve miles downstream on the west side of the river and situated such as to be easily surprised. The Indians immediately lost all interest in Hearne's survey of the river and began planning an attack by which they could steal up on the Eskimos while they slept in order to kill them. Hearne's description of the preparations and attack follow:

> It is perhaps worth remarking, that my crew, though an undisciplined rabble, and by no means accustomed to war or command, seemingly acted on this horrid occasion with utmost uniformity of sentiment. There was not among them the least altercation or separate opinion; all were united in the general cause, and ready to follow where Matonabbee led.

> Never was reciprocity of interest more generally regarded among a number of people, than it was on the present occasion by my crew, for not one was in want of any thing that another could spare; and if ever the spirit of disinterested friendship expanded the heart of a Northern Indian, it was here exhibited in the most extensive meaning of the word. Property of every kind that could be of use now ceased to be private, and every one who had any thing which came under that description, seemed proud of an opportunity of giving it, or lending it to those who had none, or were most in want of it. The number of my crew was so much greater than that which five tents could contain, and the warlike manner in which they were equipped so greatly superior to what could be expected of the poor Eskimaux, that no less than a total massacre of every one of them was likely

to be the case, unless Providence should work a miracle for their deliverance.

The land was so situated that we walked under cover of rocks and hills till we were within two hundred yards of the tents. There we lay in ambush for some time, watching the motions of the Eskimaux; and here the Indians would have advised me to stay until the fight was over, but to this I could by no means consent; for I considered that when the Eskimaux came to be surprised, they would try every way to escape and if they found me alone, not knowing me from an enemy, they would probably proceed to violence against me when no person was near me to assist. For this reason I determined to accompany them telling them at the same time, that I would not have any hand in the murder they were about to commit, unless I found it necessary for my own safety. The Indians were not displeased at this proposal; one of them immediately fixed me a spear, and another lent me a broad bayonet for my protection.

It was near one o'clock in the morning, when finding all the Eskimaux now quiet in their tents, they rushed forth from their ambuscade, and fell on the poor unsuspecting creatures, unperceived until close at the very eaves of the tents, when they soon began the bloody slaughter, while I stood neuter in the rear.

In a few seconds the horrible scene commenced; it was shocking beyond description; the poor unhappy victims were surprised in the midst of their sleep, and had neither time nor power to make any resistance; men, women and children, in all upward of twenty, ran out of their tents stark naked and endeavoured to make their escape; but the Indians having possession of all the landside, to no place could they fly for shelter. One alternative only remained, that of jumping into the river; but as none of them attempted it, they all fell a sacrifice to Indian barbarity.

The slaughter of the Eskimos by the Indians was a common occurrence in the Arctic and was usually rationalized by quoting an established superstition held by the Indians that whenever an important Northern Indian died, it was because he had been conjured to death by one of his own people, by a Southern Indian (with whom they were frequently at war), or by the Eskimos - most frequently the latter. Some protection was afforded the Eskimos by the Hudson's Bay Company with whom they traded regularly, but those who lived farther north beyond the protective influence of the Company very often fell a sacrifice to the fury and superstition of the Northern Indian.

In another instance Hearne tells how, in the summer of 1756, the Indians lay in wait at Knapp's Bay, a harbor north of the Churchill River, until the departure of the Company sloop, when they fell upon the Eskimos, killing them all. According to Hearne:

> Mr. John Bean, Master of the sloop, heard the guns very plain, but did not know the meaning or reason of it till the Summer following, when he found the shocking remains of more than forty Esquimaux who had been murdered in that cowardly manner; and for no other reason but because two principal Northern Indians had died in the preceding winter.

Hearne noted that the Indians were supremely contemptuous of the naked forms of the slaughtered Eskimo women, claiming them to be inferior to that of their own women. Nor did they make any attempt to rape or to claim the women as booty. It would appear, then, that selective mating would have prevented intermixing of the two races. This is an important point, since, although countless similar confrontations must have occurred throughout the evolutionary history of the human race, there was little merging of the two contesting groups which otherwise would have resulted in the genes of the vanquished entered the gene pool of the conquerors.

What Do These Massacres Tell Us About *Homo sapiens*?

There are two important lessons to be learned from these brutal events.

The first is that it reinforces the conclusion reached in the previous chapter that the moral imperative applies only in relations with the members of one's own in-group. Thus, in the Indians' culture, it was considered right for a stronger individual to take possessions (including wives) from weaker members of their own in-group, while the latter, for their part, were expected to relinquish their possessions. The moral imperative declared, however, that no harm should come to the participants in these contests. Even Hearne, during his earlier expeditions, was robbed, but his party otherwise left unharmed.

The Eskimo, on the other hand, were different in appearance, language, and culture to the Indians and were therefore considered to be members of the out-group. As such, the treatment of them by the Indians was exempt from any moral constraints of the type the Indians felt toward their own people and consequently they were treated as objects of derision whose massacre was considered to be a pleasurable sport - so pleasurable, in fact, that the Indians were willing to expend considerable effort in traveling long distances, and to expose themselves to dangers and hardship in their pursuit.

Furthermore, they felt no more compunction in slaughtering the Eskimos than they did in slaughtering the caribou they required for their survival. This distinction between the in-group and the out-group was obviously acceptable even to Matonabbee, a man whom we have seen to be highly altruistic in reference to his own people, but who nevertheless assumed the leadership of the expedition that massacred the Eskimo (although, according to Hearne, with some reluctance).

The second conclusion can be reached in conjunction with the consideration of two other facts. The first of these is that with the appearance of the more recent sub-species of *Homo*, a number of larger animals have become extinct. These include the mastodon, the woolly mammoth, the saber tooth tiger, the giant elk and a number of large flightless birds. We have no direct proof that humans were responsible for their demise, but there are too many instances for this to be a coincidence (see, for example: *The Sixth Extinction* by Leakey and Lewin[3]). The conclusion must be, therefore, that humans rapidly became the most powerful predator that natural selection has yet produced. This was accomplished, not by evolving enlarged fangs and claws, but by an increase in their intellectual powers that allowed humans to adapt tools as weapons, making the usual predatory accouterments unnecessary.

The second fact to be considered is that an enormous increase in complexity of the human species has occurred in a relatively short period by the usual evolutionary standards, and as we have noted, the rate of evolution is often determined by pressure imposed on a species. It seems reasonable to conclude, therefore, that in the absence of other serious predators, the pressure applied to the human species must have come from within its own ranks. In other words, competition between groups of our ancestors is the engine that has driven the more recent evolutionary changes in the human species. Any group or tribe with even a slight advantage over its competitors - as for example in the ability of its members to communicate with each other - would rapidly displace less endowed tribes. In fact a positive feeling, or pleasure, in annihilating other weaker members of the species, together with the operation of selective mating, which would reduce genetic intermixing of the two groups, would have guaranteed their survival, and would have prevented the dilution of the genes specifying such behavior. Episodes such as the Coppermine massacre must therefore have been fairly common throughout this period.

How extensive this period was, is difficult to determine, but probably corresponds to the time during which *Homo* has relied, at least partly, on hunting to satisfy his nutrient and other requirements. Evidence provided by studies of mitochondrial DNA has indicated that the most recent event in which modern humans, presumably originating in Africa, replaced their archaic ancestors, occurred about 150,000 to 250,000 years ago. This appears to have taken place worldwide, since no examples of divergent mitochondrial DNA have yet been found. In fact it is probable that such events have occurred several times previously, when, through beneficial mutations, a superior population arising at one point or another in the occupied world spread out to displace all other members of the species. The result of this process, according to the archaeological record, has been to push the frequency curve for brain size of the species toward higher values.

Displacement by Superior Variants

Although this increase appears to have occurred worldwide, it likely took place when a superior variant displaced lesser members of the species in a number of - what may be termed - **displacement waves**, spreading from a variety of locations over the area occupied by the species. Richard Leakey has likened this multi-regional evolutionary view as analogous to flinging a handful of pebbles into a pool of water, resulting in the generation of a series of ripples spreading out to encounter other ripples. Here the pool represents the area occupied by *Homo* - the entry of each pebble, the point at which there is a transition to *H sapiens* - and the ripples, their subsequent migrations.

Perhaps a more accurate analogy would replace the handful of pebbles by a light rain impinging on the pool surface so that large transitions do not occur all at once, but rather, that a series of minor transitions took place more or less sequentially and randomly over the pool surface. Each drop represents the appearance of an improved variant of *Homo*, which gradually spread outward from its point of origin eliminating lesser forms of the species as it advanced until it either occupied the entire area open to it, or encountered another more virile variant.

Hearne's vivid recounting of the supreme contempt the Indians showed for the Eskimo women during the Coppermine massacre demonstrates that if there are sufficient differences between cultures, the result is the complete annihilation of the losers. Ascribing the presence of such an attitude in *Homo sapiens sapiens* toward other subspecies (such as *Homo sapiens neaderthalensis*, for example) would provide an explanation for the absence of other variants in the DNA of modern humans.

Given the violent nature of the species, such waves would likely have spread rapidly as a particularly virile group or tribe, suddenly appearing in one location, sought to assert itself over its neighbors. The invasion of China and Eastern Europe by the Mongols, who suddenly erupted from a remote region of the Eurasian steppes, is typical of such waves. We have seen this also in the rise and fall of countless empires throughout recorded history, where a vigorous culture, ignited by the appearance of a charismatic leader, has burst forth to overwhelm its neighbors. In fact the written history of mankind is little more than a chronicle of wars. Despite the rationalizations of both apologists and historians, what purpose have the conquests of Alexander the Great, Napoleon, or Hitler served other than as an attempt to prove the superiority of one race, nation, or culture over all others?

Once again we see that humans are defined by their emotions - emotions that drive them to perform inhumane acts with the self-righteous conviction - reinforced by the rationalizations of their intellect - that such acts are justified.

Thus, as we look back through the ages at the smoldering remains of a thousand fires of genocide, we see one figure only emerging from the hanging pall - *Homo sapiens sapiens* triumphant!

The Supremacy of *H. Sapiens*

So complete is the triumph of the human species that its supremacy over other species cannot be denied. Based on its ability to displace all other species (the ultimate test of natural selection), its success is unrivaled. No other species has demonstrated a potential to annihilate humans, while humans have shown an alarming facility at annihilating others. It is even within our power to sterilize the planet - either by intention or by accident!

The fact of our supremacy is denied by many who feel that by admitting to being "at the top of the heap," we would be prone to arrogance. Such a situation should not inspire arrogance, however, but rather *awe* when contemplating the terrible powers we have garnered, and *humility* upon recognition of our proven fallibility!

Violence Toward Others Is Common in All Races and Cultures

The pleasure that we feel in violent behavior towards others whom we have designated as members of the out-group is certainly not lacking in modern humans. The truth of this is evident in the popularity of the large number of violent episodes depicted in the mass media. In the recent tribal wars in Rwanda, one youth, when asked why he participated in the massacre of women and children seeking sanctuary in a church, had a simple answer, saying in effect: "Because it was fun!"

There have been countless instances in recent history in which one race or tribe has abused or slaughtered another. These include holy wars, tribal wars, the slave trade, the displacement of native peoples from their traditional grounds, and even the demands for capital punishment of those who have been labeled enemies of the state. The worst of such episodes have been notable for their ability to generate such blatant euphemisms as: "The final solution" and "Ethnic cleansing." Even after the abolition of slavery, the privileged classes in Europe continued to treat servants with contempt and even physical abuse of a type that they would not consider inflicting on the members of their own class.

In fact no race or culture is exempt, since many who have been victims in certain cases of persecution, have themselves been the perpetrators in others. We have just seen that the North American Indians, who were slaughtered, driven from their land, and treated with supreme contempt by the Europeans, had traditionally treated the Eskimo in the same manner. The African Negroes, who were frequently victims of the slave trade, have repeatedly engaged in slaughter of other black members of rival tribes. Even the Jews, who have suffered persecution for thousands of years, culminating in the recent and most exaggerated attempt at racial extinction, are not exempt. In city after city during their conquest of the promised land, they were ordered by Yahweh, their traditional god, to

> strike every living creature with the edge of the sword and leave none alive.

Typical is Yahweh's order for revenge on the Amalekites:

> go and smite Amalek, and utterly destroy all that they have, and spare them not; but slay both man and woman, infant and suckling, ox, sheep, camel and ass (1 Samuel 15:3).

This order was obeyed by Saul, who

> smote the Amalekites from Havilah until thou comest to Shur, by the sword (ibid verse 8).

Thus, as has been amply demonstrated throughout history, the group concept makes it possible for any tribe or nation to be readily aroused to actions of violence against another group by the emotional appeals of leaders who usually exploit differences involving nationalism, religion, culture, and race.

Tribes as Gene Pools

The tribes or groups into which early humans organized themselves became, in essence, gene pools. Thus, competition between tribes was actually competition between gene pools, and we may conclude that during this stage in human evolution, natural selection was acting on gene pools as well as on individuals.

Mutations would still have occurred in individuals, however, and through them the resulting genes would have been introduced into the gene pool. If these genes resulted in a superior individual (as, for example, one with increased reasoning power or a greater ability to communicate) that individual would tend to be dominant in his or her tribe and as a consequence, to have more mates and more offspring than the less dominant members.

But to gain status in the group the superior member would have had an advantage if she or he had another trait - a drive to rise in the esteem of the other members of the group, a goal she or he could attain by exploiting her or his superior qualities. In fact, such an urge would have been an advantage to every member in attaining mates, which is why most present-day humans strive to increase their own rank in today's societies.

Another trait which most of the members probably possessed was a tendency to **adulate** - *a willingness to recognize the superiority of certain members and to assign them a position of authority, thus allowing the tribe to benefit from the qualities of such a leader.* That this trait is still present in the species today is evident in the number of emperors, kings, sultans, dictators, etc. whom, throughout history, have been granted virtually absolute power, or in many cases, deified. Even in today's more sophisticated nations, with their efficient communication systems which reveal the mortality and blemishes of their leaders, people continue to admire those having superior physical qualities such as sport champions and beauty queens, or intellectual prowess, such as artists, writers, musicians and even scientists.

Thus, superior genes would have proliferated within the gene pool and would have provided an advantage to the recipient tribe over its neighbors.

More aggressive tribes would tend to eliminate less aggressive tribes, so that the presence of combative genes in a pool would also give that pool an advantage. In fact a positive stimulus such as pleasure in destroying competitors would, as we have seen, soon appeared.

At the same time, excessive aggression would have been a disadvantage as it could endanger members of the tribe and diminish the attention paid to other important functions, such as caring for dependents. Those tribes that attained an optimum balance between aggressiveness and restraint would prosper since they would have been favored by natural selection.

Once more we should stress that members of a successful tribe would also have had to possess an important quality - a genuine feeling of altruism - a desire to treat other members of their own tribe with respect and concern. This would have been an essential factor in promoting the cohesion of the tribe. As we have seen, such 'moral restraint' would have only applied to members of their own tribe, however, and would have been suspended in dealings with others outside the tribe, particularly the 'enemy'. Killing a member of the tribe would have been a sin, while killing an enemy - laudable.

All of this supports the conclusion reached in the previous chapter that it is the function of the genes to provide us with emotional concepts such as 'the in-group' and 'the out-group'. Defining the composition or membership of these groups is the function of learning (or imprinting), which we acquire through experience and through the examples provided by our parents and our culture.

The Importance of the Genetic Component
The importance of environment and genetics in defining the in-group is exemplified by the two main characters in the Coppermine massacre - Matonabbee and Hearne himself. Both were men of heroic proportions, but who differed in the scope of the concept each had of his own in-group. Matonabbee was highly egoistic and nationalistic, confining his allegiance mainly to his own race. Hearne, on the other

hand, was more humane in that he appeared to include the species as a whole in his in-group concept. No doubt learning and environment played a large part in this difference, but the genetic component of the personalities of the two men seemed to dominate the differences. One has the feeling that had the two men been brought up in each other's culture, they would have acted more or less the same as they had in their own culture.

We are thus left with a very important question: what is the origin of the differences in the cultures of these two men? This will be the theme of the next chapter.

References

1. Samuel Hearne. "A Journey from Prince of Wales Fort in Hudson's Bay to the Northern Ocean in the Years 1769, 1770, 1771 and 1772," with introduction, notes, and illustrations by J. B. Tyrrell, The Champlain Society, Toronto, 1911.

2. Samuel Hearne. "Coppermine Journey, An Account of a Great Adventure - selected from the journals of Samuel Hearne by Farley Mowat," Published by McClelland & Stewart Ltd. Copyright by Farley Mowat, Canada, 1958.

3. Leakey, R., and R. Lewin. The Sixth Extinction: Patterns of Life and the Future of Humankind. New York: Doubleday. 1995.

CHAPTER EIGHT

EUROPEAN CIVILIZATIONS

In the previous chapter, we saw an example of a northern hunter-gather society. Although this society was located in North America, similar societies probably existed in prehistoric northern Eurasia as well, as the recent discovery of the 'Iceman' in an Alpine glacier seems to indicate. We must ask, then: "How was the population of Europe transformed over the past ten thousand years from a strictly hunter-gatherer lifestyle into its present urbanized society, while the population of northern North America remained essentially unaltered over this same period?" Or, more briefly: "Why did humans first start to form cities and states?" Let us, in what follows, consider one possible outline of events which might have led to such a change.

The Development of Agriculture

As the most recent ice age approached and the glaciers advanced in what is now Europe, the inhabitants were driven south, causing an increase in the population density of Asia Minor. This produced a shortage of food available to the hunter-gatherer societies occupying this area and caused them to adopt a more agrarian lifestyle.

It is usually stated that farming was 'invented' in Asia Minor, but the idea of taking some of the grain that had been gathered and spreading it over a previously cleared plot of land is so obvious that it must have been pursued many times and at many places during human history. This would have been true of animal husbandry as well since on many occasions humans must have reared animals to be used as a source of food and clothing. However, provided adequate food could be obtained by hunting and gathering, such activities were probably not worthwhile.

But, as the pressure imposed on the populace by crowding increased during the Ice-age, the frequency of planned crop growth and rearing of animals would, of necessity, also have increased. The most fertile areas for crop growth were concentrated along river valleys, such as those of the Tigris, Euphrates, Nile, and Indus rivers, and it was here that the earliest agricultural settlements arose.

The perfecting of these practices probably resulted from the members of the tribe experimenting to determine the best methods of growing, harvesting and storing crops, as well as attempting to determine the best species to be cultivated. So too with animals, the most suitable species to tame and the techniques for their care would also have been investigated. The information gained in this way would have been passed on to the younger generations and become part of the persistent wisdom of these tribes. We may conclude, then, that agriculture was not invented, but rather, was perfected in the Middle East due to the food demands of a higher population density.

The Separation of Hunter-Gathers from Agrarians

As the glaciers slowly receded toward the north, more land once again became available for hunting and gathering, and the populace again spread into the rest of what is now Europe. History shows that the practice of farming was not abandoned entirely to hunting and gathering, however. Instead, farming continued to flourish in the Middle East from where it slowly spread west and north over a period of several thousand years, ultimately covering most of the arable land in what is now Europe. We see, then, that the population of Europe was, at one time, divided into two cultures - the **agrarians** and the **hunter-gathers**. These two modes of living required different behavioral patterns. The successful agrarian would be an individual who would be content to remain stationary and to establish a permanent residence, while hunter-gathers would be more restless and happier ranging widely in search of food. The agrarian would feel a compulsion to plan ahead and to fill his time in fruitful labor, and would pursue his goals with a single-minded determination.

By contrast, the hunter-gatherers would not concern themselves with far-reaching plans and would find constant surroundings and activities boring and distasteful since, as we saw in the last chapter, for those depending on hunting or gathering to supply their needs, wide ranges are a necessity. Furthermore, being predators, when food was in short supply, they would not hesitate to raid the agrarian communities, who in turn would be forced to organize and form larger more coherent groups for protection.

The Two Cultures Show Behavioral Differences

An important difference between the agrarian and hunter-gatherers is the view each society has of ownership - in particular, the ownership of land. While hunter-gatherers may have a vague concept of their right to range over a large area with others of their tribe, the successful agrarians require smaller but more discrete plots, which they feel they alone have the right to occupy. Thus, the concepts of 'possessions' and 'rights' have a more vivid meaning to the agrarian.

Another notable distinction between the two cultures arises from their divergent concept of authority. W. B. Miller[1] has studied the differences between this concept as held by urbanized European society and by the native North American hunter-gatherers.

The European View of Authority

Miller points out that the European society is essentially hierarchal and may be viewed as a pyramid, with the supreme power issuing from the top. This is best illustrated by the Christian religion, which places God at the pinnacle, with a host of supernatural beings ranged under Him, and beneath them power is passed to the worldly elements headed by a pope or clergy who mediate and direct the power toward the common masses. Order in society is maintained by the temporal establishment, which is sanctioned and given divine authority through the clergy. At its peak this was epitomized by the doctrine of royal absolutism, which stated that the king or monarch was sacred because he was anointed by the priests and it was therefore blasphemy and sacrilege to assail his person or conspire against him. Since he was an earthly image of God's majesty, it was considered wrong to look upon him as a mere man. Although we reject the concept of the divine nature of our leaders today, as Miller notes, we have nevertheless been witness recently to

> obsessive extremes in the hysteria of massed tribute to Hitler, Mussolini, and Queen Elizabeth; the screaming adulation of adolescent girls to a popular singer; the frenzy of a Broadway reception for General MacArthur, and the passionate devotion of a cult group to its leader.

Miller also points out, that on a more mundane level, Europeans continue to utilize many terms implying superior-subordinate role-relationships, such as master-servant, officer-enlisted man, boss-employee, teacher-pupil, parent-child, doctor-patient, captain-crew, etc. These relationships are accepted as normal and necessary for the proper functioning of the various institutions composing society, as well as for society itself. Through these relationships, one individual is empowered to direct the action of others over whom he is accorded greater prestige.

This inequality of status is affirmed by the behavior of the inferior who may salute, bow, stand at attention, wait to be addressed before speaking and who may address the superior as: "Sir," "Mister," "Doctor." or "Your honor." As a sort of equivalent to 'royal trappings' the superior will frequently assume a dress that distinguishes him from the inferior, as the officer does from the enlisted man and the executive from the laborer.

The European's concept of 'status' carries with it the connotation of 'height'. Thus a person having authority will be described as 'high-ranking', 'upper-class', or 'on top', while those of little authority are 'underlings', 'down and out,' or 'members of the lower class'. This, of course, is consistent with the view of most organizations as being pyramidal. The European concept of 'power', on the other hand, tends to be reified, to be conceived of as a liquid-like substance that flows down through the various levels of authority, with the upper levels having a greater capacity and therefore containing a larger amount of power. In summarizing European society, Miller states that

> The vertical authority relationship is a fundamental building block of European society. Without it the phenomenon of 'ranked' authority - where given individuals are permanently empowered to direct others - would be impossible, and ranked authority is an indispensable feature of European organizational systems.

The Indian View of Authority

Having dealt with the Europeans, Miller next turns to the Fox Indians, whose history and lifestyle are the best documented of all the tribes of the Algonkian nation. He begins by quoting several observations made by European visitors to North America in the seventeenth and eighteenth centuries concerning their contacts with the tribes occupying the western Great Lakes region. All these observers were struck by the fact that there seemed to be no central religious, political, or military authority, yet the natives proved to be extremely effective hunters and fighters. All agreed that, as one observer put it (ca 1680),

> Subordination is not a maxim among these savages (who do) not know what it is to obey....It is more necessary to entreat him than to command him....The father does not venture to exercise authority over his son, nor does the chief dare give commands to his soldiers. [quoted by Miller],

and according to another:

> the savages...think it unaccountable that one man should have more than another, and that the rich should have more respect than the poor; they value themselves above anything you can imagine, and this is the reason they always give for it - that one man's as much master as another, and since all men are made of the same clay, there should be no distinction or superiority among them. [quoted by Miller].

Concerning the feasibility of recruiting them as soldiers, this was considered impractical since, as one French recruiter notes

> these people have no idea of royal grandeur nor majesty, nor of the power of superiors over inferiors, and thus would not feel among themselves any emulation or ambition to reach these... honors, and consequently no desire

to perform their duties. Neither would they be influenced thereto by fear of punishment, for, not tolerating any among themselves, they would suffer still less that others should inflict any on them.

I am persuaded that if any [French] captain would give some command to the subaltern officers or soldiers of his [Indian] company, they would tell him curtly that they would not do it, and to let him do it himself. That would, verily, be a fine example for French troops! [quoted by Miller],

while his English counterpart remarks:

Although [the Indians] have both military and civil chiefs, yet [they] are sensible of neither civil nor military subordination. As every one of them entertains a very high opinion of his consequence, and is extremely tenacious of his liberty, all injunctions that carry with them the appearance of a command are instantly rejected with scorn. On this account it is seldom that their leaders are so indiscrete as to give out orders in a peremptory style...there is no visible form of government; they allow of no such distinction as [that between] magistrate and subject, everyone appearing to enjoy an independence that cannot be controlled... [quoted by Miller].

These observations of Indian society were obviously biased by the condescending attitudes of the Europeans who judged the society of the "savages" in terms of their own. Such condescension assumes ironical proportions, however, when one considers how the Europeans came to idealize the golden age of ancient Greece - in particular, commending the democratic qualities of its society - while at the same time ignoring the presence of this philosophy amongst the Indians. All three societies denied women their democratic rights and employed slaves (whom the Europeans preferred to call servants). In spite of these failings, however, the fact is that equality of rights applied to a far larger segment of the Indian society than either of the other more 'advanced' cultures!

In the Fox religion, there is a host of supernatural beings with whom mortals deal one-on-one; there is no priesthood or other mediating agency. The essential feature of religious thought revolves around 'manitu', or supernatural power. Any being may possess it - but only temporarily, as with the 'luck' of a gambler. To succeed is to have manitu; to fail is to have lost it. As none can have permanent claim to it, none can have enduring superiority over all others - thus there is no hierarchy in the Fox religion.

There were positions of authority in the Fox society, but these had the interesting feature that the power their incumbents wielded was inversely proportional to the length of their tenure. The tribal chief, for example, obtained his office hereditarily and usually for life, but his power was limited to conducting meetings at which he was expected only to act as arbiter and peacemaker in the event of dissension. A war leader was usually chosen only when a military expedition was contemplated.

We saw that this was true also of the Chipewyans in the previous chapter where Matonabee's leadership lasted only for the duration of the massacre and during his diplomatic forays into Cree territory. In spite of the considerable stature he enjoyed amongst his countrymen, not once does Hearne refer to Matonabee as: "Captain," or "Chief." In both the Fox and Chipewyan societies, the leader's power was limited to suggesting courses of action, which individuals could accept or reject as they desired. His incumbency lasted only for the duration of the expedition, and in the Fox society, the leader was not allowed to reenter the village until after a ceremony in which his authority was vividly and symbolically revoked. The tribe also had a ceremony leader whose function was restricted to conducting religious rituals in a traditional manner.

Miller characterizes the Fox individual as being highly moral and assuming individual responsibility for knowing and acting in accordance with the regulations of his society. An order to a Fox was considered to be an insult since it implied that he was inadequate in the knowledge and performance of traditional rules of correct behavior.

Miller also points out that English society of the sixth century resembled the Algonkian society of the sixteenth century in many ways. It was organized on a tribal basis of roughly the same size of political units; it was at the same technological level and was preoccupied with intertribal warfare. By contrast, however, the average warrior of the English - and Germanic tribes in general - displayed an obsessive loyalty to the clan chief, considering it an act of infamy to survive the chief in battle and a life long duty to seek vengeance in the event of his death.

Attitudes Unchanged Today

The rejection of authority by the Fox tribe appears to be inherent, since Miller has remarked: "that even today - 300 years later - organized activity appears to proceed in the absence of any visible authority."

So too are the attitudes of the Europeans essentially unchanged today - even those living in North America - as the researches of Stanley Milgram[2] have shown. The experiments he and his associates performed demonstrated that, using their authority, the directors of the research project were able to order volunteers (who were in fact the subjects of the experiment), to apply apparently painful electric shocks to those they assumed to be the true subjects. The latter were actually conspirators, who received no shocks at all, but only acted as though they were in great pain. The volunteers responded to orders by applying increasingly higher apparent voltages, even though they themselves were visibly distressed by the results of their own actions. These actions were not sadistic but rather were prompted by a deference to authority, which in their eyes overruled what would otherwise be a normal sympathetic response.

The Differences Appear To Be the Result of Gene Refluxing

I have outlined the characteristics of the arch-typical agrarian and hunter-gatherer personalities. There is no doubt a cultural basis for the difference in the conduct of the members of these two societies, but this would be unlikely to persist over long intervals of time in the absence of an underlying genetic dissimilarity, especially in the Americas where the two cultures have been forced into intimate contact. We must conclude, therefore, that such differences must arise essentially from basic, although minor, genetic differences.

Few individuals in either culture would be wholly of one type or the other. In fact the genes of all these characteristics would be present in most individuals in both societies, but in post-glacial Europe, through the agency of gene refluxing, the frequency of specific genes would become greater in one society or the other. For example, a person of restless nature born in a mainly agrarian society, might under the weight of cultural strictures attempt to conform. He would not be able to do so comfortably, however, since it would violate his innate nature. Thus, given the choice, he would be more likely to join others of like preferences to leave the community and live a more nomadic life. A similar drift in the opposite direction would tend to move sedentary individuals, and their behavioral genes, back into the agrarian society. Thus we see that the separation of the population of Europe into two behaviorally distinct forms of society, following the retreat of the glaciers, is a typical case of gene refluxing.

The submissive characteristic of the agrarians made it possible for them to form protective associations to counter the threat of hunter-gatherer raids. Those agrarians having all the traits that promote socialization, tended to aggregate to form larger and more cohesive communities, providing themselves with a greater chance of survival as compared to those refusing the protection of such communities. Thus genes promoting pious submissive concepts flourished in the agrarian societies, allowing them to organize into larger communities - and ultimately - nations.

Fidelity concepts were not lacking in the hunter-gatherer societies, however, since these promote the welfare of the tribes. On the other hand, large communities would not be an advantage in their way of life, which would function optimally at a lower population density, as we saw in the previous chapter.

Although there would have been periods of gene fractionation during which distinct populations of agrarians and hunter-gatherers formed, there were also periods of melding, when, due to changes in population density or food supply, one population was forced to invade the territory of the other. This resulted in the mixing of individuals from the two populations and a subsequent reversal of gene refluxing. In effect, the separate niches occupied by the two populations disappeared during this period, so that new subspecies or even new races were never formed. This temporary reversal of gene refluxing was sporadic at first, but over the long term, the agrarians prevailed, due to their larger population, better organization and greater resources. Perhaps the final hunter-gatherer holdouts in Europe were the Vikings who continued to raid other cultures until comparatively recent times.

The Dominance of the Agrarians in Europe

Thus, following the retreat of the glaciers, the agrarian communities slowly but inexorably expanded to the west and north, taking over the ranges of the hunter-gatherers who were either exterminated or forced to live in the agrarian society. Here many succumbed to smallpox, tuberculosis, syphilis, and other diseases endemic in large, dense communities, to which the long-time residents had largely become immune. The overall result of this process was that the gradual increase in population density - which favored the agrarians - brought about an increase in the frequency of genes for agrarian behavior in the general population of Europe.

Following the absorption of the hunter-gatherers, gene fractionation came to an end, with the gene frequencies fixed approximately at what we see today. Since each of these genetic variations is present - or is expressed to a different extent - in each individual, there is a statistical distribution of the behavioral traits amongst different individuals in the general population. The core of European society thus consists of a majority of pious, single-minded, hard-working, possessive individuals prepared to submit to authority, and a smaller number of restless individuals high in hunter-gatherer traits, who, given the opportunity, would leave the rigid community of the agrarians in whose society they are misfits.

There are also present in European society a number of individuals who, while being as determined and single-minded as the agrarians, are at the same time inclined to be as aggressive and predatory as the hunter-gatherers. Amongst these individuals are the political and religious leaders, entrepreneurs, and army officers, who organize and govern society, forming an elite class that associates mainly with other similar individuals, confining their breeding mainly to their own class. In fact this tendency to breed within the community of like individuals, and thus form classes within society, does provide some fractionation of genes, but does little to alter the overall gene frequency. Those genes specifying the agrarians mentality predominate, however, and one can see it expressed in today's society in what might be termed: "The clipped lawn syndrome." This is an almost fanatical desire for neatness and order causing the members of European communities (whether in Europe or not) to become incensed by neighbors who are negligent in so minor a duty as keeping their lawns trimmed!

The Industrial Revolution

Eventually, due to population increase, the European consumption of food began to outstrip its production and more efficient means of food production and distribution were required. This led to the Industrial Revolution, which was fired by enterprising individuals, but whose mainstay was the agrarian majority. These latter individuals, in turn, accepted their position as willing workers, transferring readily from the fields to the factories. All the traits that promoted the agricultural revolution now drove its industrial equivalent - a pious acceptance of authority; a feeling of righteousness in performing the work - which in their minds assumed the status of a 'duty' - and a need for the security provided to them as members of a large coherent group of fellow workers.

All these feelings were further enhanced by religious and nationalistic teachings. If they were victims, they were willing victims, since no amount of coercion could have convinced so many individuals, if unwilling, to spend virtually their entire lives in one activity. For this to be possible, there had to be an innate feeling amongst them of security in a structured and - to them - meaningful life inherent in each of the workers. Thus gene refluxing has transformed mankind to the point where the statement frequently made, that: "The man on the moon is no different to the man on the tundra." is invalid.

Gene Refluxing in Asia

While all this was happening in Europe, similar selective migrations were taking place in Asia. Here again, the glacial advance compressed the population, mainly along river valleys, forcing an adoption of an agrarian lifestyle followed by a subsequent efflux of the hunter-gatherer component as the ice sheets receded. In this case, however, a much larger range lay open to the hunter-gatherers. This came about because of a land bridge between Asia and North America, which appeared, in what is now the Bering Straits, due to a drop in sea level, caused in turn when large amounts of water were withdrawn from the oceans to form the glacial ice fields. So vast was this new territory of the Americas that the Asiatic agrarians did not catch up with the migrants before the land bridge disappeared. Nor did the population density of the hunter-gatherers now located in the Americas increase to the point where a serious shift to agriculture was necessary - except in one region - that of the confines of Central America and a few river valleys in the northern Andes mountains, where a succession of incipient agrarian civilizations arose. This occurred at a much later date than its equivalent in Europe, however.

The Age of Colonization

With the rise of influence of the European nations came the age of imperialism when expeditions were sent out to exploit areas beyond continental Europe. The discovery of the Americas provided a vast opportunity for the entrepreneurs of the European maritime nations who deployed armies and colonists over the newly discovered territories. The indigenous populations of this new world consisted mainly of hunter-gatherer tribes and the relatively young agrarian societies in the region of Central America. None of the natives had been subjected to the stress and selective pressures produced by large population density to the same extent - and over the same length of time - as the colonists, and, as a consequence, had not experienced a mechanical revolution. They were therefore defenseless against the products of the Europeans' own high population density - their diseases, caused by urban living - and their weapons, produced in response to the competitive nature of their homeland.

Agrarian Dominance

The spread of the European population in the Americas has been typical of countless other expansions of dominant populations throughout human history, during which the culture with the advantage simply overwhelms the less advantaged, killing, enslaving, and displacing their members from their traditional foraging areas in a purely detached fashion. Following the usual evolutionary script, the holocaust perpetrated on the

American aboriginals would in time have seen the extinction of their less organized societies. However, the more humane elements in the European populace have, for the moment, succeeded in restraining these activities.

Some members of the hunter-gatherer populace have joined the fringes of European society, becoming teachers, lawyers, doctors and other professionals. The patronizing champions of the aboriginal within the European community have pointed to these individuals as proof that they, in their words: "are just as intelligent as we." In fact intelligence is not the issue since there is no evidence of intellectual differences between the races. The real difference lies in the attitudes and goals of the average member of each society; the inherent ant-like behavioral characteristics of the Europeans allows them to organize in larger and more powerful groups, which easily overwhelmed the more scattered aboriginal tribes. The differences between these two variants are minor, but minor advantages are all that is needed to give one variant or race physical ascendancy over another. This gives a new meaning to the evolutionary term 'fitness' - the **fittest variant** *is simply the one that displaces all others, and is for the moment, dominant.* Through a series of such displacements, a species is gradually altered over long periods of time. The fossil record, being sparse and sporadic, seldom gives more than an episodic account of this grand panorama, however.

The majority of aboriginals are not interested in joining the agrarian society and despise those of their race who do, sometimes referring to them as "apples" (red outside and white inside). Their main goal is to return to the life they once enjoyed, and for the moment, they entertain some hope of doing so. As the pressures of population growth and global shortage of resources continues to bear on the world's nations, however, the proponents of racial purity will inevitably gain ascendancy once more and the racial wars will be revived. Perhaps we have already seen the initiation of this phase of history with the emergence of the 'bunker America' rationale - the visceral worship of God and guns - that has, from time to time, induced the formation of armed defense groups throughout North America. These groups are typical of many under pressure in which the conservative elements have risen to the fore by proclaiming that hostile forces threaten them. Even their own government has betrayed them in their eyes and therefore - they reason - there is no longer a moral requirement to obey its edicts.

Finally we might note that the relatively sudden appearance of, first agricultural and then technological societies, can be seen (according to the above proposed scheme of events) to be the result of local increases in population density. Such increases had probably not occurred during the previous 200,000 years of modern humans' history, simply because of an initially low total global population and a previously unlimited territory into which the increasing population could expand. Thus, I maintain, modern societies are not the product of an increasing intellectual ability, but rather of a change in the goals, and hence the overall behavior, of the members of those societies.

References

1. Miller, W.B. "Two Concepts of Authority," American Anthropologist, 57:271-89 1955.

2. Milgram, Stanley. Obedience to Authority: An Experimental View. New York: Harper & Row, 1974.

CHAPTER NINE

SEX, RELIGION AND MORAL BEHAVIOR

Male Dominance

The female animal is limited in the number of pregnancies she is able to experience during her lifetime. The male, on the other hand, is virtually unlimited in the number of individuals he is able to sire. Thus it is that the female's investment in each pregnancy is greater than the male's and as a consequence it is in her interest to be discriminating and to resist advances from unsuitable males in the hope of ultimately attracting a more suitable one.

The male who attempts to force himself on a female he considers desirable will be more successful in doing so if his chosen mate is smaller and weaker than he. This means that over time, the smaller females will have been in a pregnant state more frequently than their larger or more powerful sisters - a circumstance which will have resulted in an increase in the genes for weaker females and more powerful and dominant males. The more successful males will, in turn, be those who are attracted to smaller females.

The weakening of the females will continue with each generation, but will not continue indefinitely since a female who is too weak would be unable to protect her young. Thus it is that a functional optimum in the relative sizes of the sexes will have been established by natural selection in most mammals.

The actual male/female-size ratio for each species is a product of its *modus vivendi.* In the case of the gorilla, for instance, the male is highly protective of his family. As a result, his mates are small and the size ratio for this animal is high. The female bear, on the other hand, is left to care for her young entirely on her own and is therefore closer in size to the male.

Humans are highly social animals whose young enjoy the protection, not only of the males, but of the whole group to which they belong. The successful male, then, can afford to mate with females who are weaker than he is and more vulnerable to his advances - and it is for this reason that men are generally attracted to smaller, more slender women.

The successful female, in turn, assumes a vulnerable appearance by such means as wearing skirts. That this apparel suggests vulnerability is evident when one notes that the male finds a 'mini-skirt' to be more seductive than shorts of the same length!

In general, men accept their superior role as a divine right, justifying it with the argument that God (Who, as the most dominant being must be male) willed that it be so - otherwise He would not have made it so! This argument is promulgated by all the major religions, allowing them to subjugate their female adherents and to exclude them from most positions of authority in the religious hierarchy.

Women, for their part, tend to accept their inferior position as being part of the "natural order of things" and therefore "God ordained." Many are uncomfortable when a man is not in any position of authority, which is why there have been so few elected female heads-of-state. It also explains in part why women find those men attractive who display competence and success and why they prefer that the male takes charge of their relationships. This attitude reduces friction within a group and therefore contributes to the success of the species.

But Why Monogamy?

There is much evidence suggesting that as early humans emerged from a strictly arboreal confine they extended their provisioning activities from that of gathering alone, to include hunting as well. This activity appears to have been enhanced by a change to an erect posture, which increased the distance they were able to see, allowing them to hunt across the savannah. It also freed their hands, augmenting their ability to use weapons and to fashion tools. These skills in turn, were enhanced by an increase in reasoning power which occurred at the same time

The increase in reasoning power and the availability of the hands for manipulating objects, if developed individually, would have increased the success of the species, but in concert, their effect was synergistic, multiplying the advantage many times. Thus it may have been, that a change in posture was the catalyst for the relatively rapid increase in human intelligence.

Hunting required the hunters - mainly men - to become more aggressive and willing to range more widely from their home base - while the women, encumbered by children, remained closer to home engaged in the ancestral occupation of gathering. The successful male was one whose every expenditure of energy was directed toward the nurturing of his own progeny, which meant that he had to avoid being cuckolded during his absence on hunting expeditions. The successful male, therefore, was one who felt the urge to obtain a mate who, in his judgment, would be faithful to him during his absence. The successful female, in turn, sought the security of a dependable male which was more readily accomplished by those having a propensity towards dependability themselves. Thus on the part of both sexes a genuine overt inherent devotion toward each other would have proved advantageous, and in turn led to the selection in humans of a tendency toward fidelity between couples.

Individuals who felt this urge would have benefitted by association with others of the same compulsion, and as a consequence, monogamy, which promotes harmony within a group, became associated in a positive sense with the group concept and led to a taboo against promiscuity. In most societies, this communal interest usually leads to the sanctioning by the group or society of monogamous unions, which are usually ritualized through the performance of marriage ceremonies.

But Not *Too* Much Monogamy!

For the man, however, there was, at the same time, an advantage in surreptitiously cuckolding other men, who would then be deceived into providing for his offspring. The female, for her part, occasionally found it in her interest to transfer her affections to a more promising mate. Consequently, the tendency toward monogamy did not become an obsession, but through the operation of natural selection reached a functional optimum - an intensity amongst the early hunter-gatherers that is close to that found in today's society.

As with other forces in behavior imposed on humans by natural selection, the sexual urge does not reach the same level of intensity in each individual, but rather has a statistical distribution within the population. This means that all individuals do not feel the urge toward monogamy or promiscuity with average intensity, but rather that the intensity of each urge varies from individual to individual. So it is that within society there is a whole gamut of sexual behaviors, from highly monogamous to highly promiscuous - with the largest number of individuals feeling these urges at, or near, average intensity. This accounts for the fluid nature of sexual mores, which are defined by the constantly changing influence various groups of individuals are able to exert within society at any instant.

One of the effects of these influences is that women proclaim their modesty by averting their eyes from those of unfamiliar males. Men, on the other hand, openly assess each female they encounter to determine her suitability as a possible sexual partner, by noting the degree to which she conforms to their concept of the ideal female. They remain rapists at heart despite the restraints imposed on them by the requirements of membership in their social group and, as a consequence, are the more frequent initiators of the sexual act, to which the female is usually acquiescent. She may exhibit some initial reluctance, however, when first approached by an unfamiliar male, allowing her time to assess the suitability of the interested male.

Religion

Communal living is absolutely essential for the survival of our species, since the strength, speed and offensive weapons possessed by individual humans compare so badly with those of other animals. It is imperative, therefore, that - for their own safety and that of their offspring - individual humans join a group of other humans who are dedicated to the protection of all.

To be a member of such a group requires that those attempting to join possess qualities that contribute to their role as functioning members of the group . These qualities include:

- **Gregariousness** - the desire for the company of others.
- **Skepticism** - to avoid being host to cheaters
- **Altruism** - to avoid being themselves labeled 'cheaters' by exhibiting a *genuine* concern for the welfare of others.
- **Loyalty** to the group which they are openly prepared to defend against all threats.

Each of these qualities, or characteristics, is expressed with an intensity which varies amongst members of the population. Thus, if we were able to measure this intensity in each individual, and to plot this data in the usual fashion, we would be provided with the usual bell-shaped curve - which is to say that all members of a society are not committed to the society to the same extent.

So important are these qualities, that most successful individuals feel them profoundly - so profoundly in fact, that their concept of "the group" is as a beneficent and powerful entity whose authority is paramount! It is this concept of the **Supreme Authority** which is viewed by many as real and absolute. Furthermore, this concept demands of its possessors - not only that they believe in it - but that they *want* to believe in it and to resist all attempts to prove its existence to be false!

Through imprinting and parental guidance this concept merges with that of the group to which we belong to form the **Communal** or **Group Concept** and it is this concept, which we personify as "God," or "the Nation."

Is God a lie told by our genes to compel us to act in ways that increase our biological success?

The answer to this question is, almost certainly: "Yes." But it is not important to our welfare whether God exists, or does not exist. What *is* important, is that we submit to the demands imposed on our behavior by the concept - whether we believe the reason for doing so is in obedience to the edicts of a Supreme Being, in response to our natural feelings or simply because we consider such behavior to be prudent and noble.

Religion may be defined as **the objectification of the communal concept and its personification as the Supreme Being** (variously termed Allah, God, Jehovah, the Creator, etc.).

We see, then, that religion arises from a need to submit to our preconception of 'the group' as 'something greater than ourselves' and that responding to this emotional need has contributed to the establishment of societies, and hence, to the survival of modern *Homo sapiens*. Through it we are driven to promote our own gene pool and hence the genes that specify this preconception. Because of it, we are possessed with an inherent desire to be accepted by our compatriots and to treat them with consideration and respect, acting toward them in a morally commendable, and frequently altruistic, fashion - and why we feel a powerful allegiance to the social groups to which we belong.

It is also true that religion has had a profound influence on history and still forms an integral part of every culture. Furthermore, because of its emotional nature, it has inspired some of the most intensely satisfying works of art.

At the same time as we acknowledge these benefits, however, we cannot ignore the confrontational aspect of religion, which has promoted our species by urging it to eliminate all competition. This urge is evident in the slogans it inspires: "The one true faith," "The chosen people," "Onward Christian soldiers!" "death to the infidel!" and in the many holy wars, crusades, jihads, pogroms, fatwahs, persecutions, inquisitions and slaughters it has motivated throughout history.

In spite of the recent enormous increase in the rational powers of our species, we still persist in allowing the emotional appeal of religion to overcome our reason. We ignore the harm it has done in the past and the dangers it presents for the future. We have faith. We know that God exists in the very depths of our beings. We persist in the claim that without a belief in God there can be no foundation for moral behavior and as a consequence, without this conviction we would all be subject to "The laws of the jungle." All religions promulgate this fiction, stating that religious teachings promote decent behavior. The reverse is true, however, and it is *because* most humans are already basically decent, that religious institutions are possible!

We insist on rationalizing the existence of God. Each of us is convinced of the authenticity of her or his own concept of God, Who, we contend, is an absolute that exists beyond our own conscious selves. Much intellectual energy has been expended in discussing the 'true nature' of God without arriving at any consensus, which is hardly surprising since each person's concept of this 'Supreme Power' is purely subjective - a product of her or his own individual experience, imprinting and genetic makeup.

The concept of God most of us have, is (as we have already stated) simply a personification of the group concept, which instills in us the feeling that by accepting the supremacy of the group and committing ourselves to it, we are promised security for ourselves and our families.

We speak of the 'soul' as our spiritual selves, which our egos demand must be immortal - since our bodies are obviously not! But is the soul really anything more than our emotional selves? I believe that most rational humans realize that the existence of a personal God - a Superior

Being imbued with human desires and urges (such as love, jealousy and vengefulness) is basically irrational.

At the same time, however, we all possess - to a greater or lesser intensity - the feeling that there is a 'force greater than ourselves' to which we owe reverence and loyalty and which many of us personify as God or 'the nation'. Those having this certainty, sustain it with **faith - a desire to believe in the face of rational rejection.**

Many of us 'have faith', which we regard as accepting this force as actual and viewing the accompanying feelings and concepts as innate or revealed knowledge. So important is our acceptance of the supremacy of this force to our success, that our genes cause us to experience a powerful emotional need to promote and defend its validity.

But perhaps we should not be too severe in our condemnation of religion, which, after all, along with nationalism and **racism**, is only the symptom of a compulsion - an urge that obliges its victims to promote their own culture at all costs - an urge we might term **ethnophilia**, *the imperative to advance belligerently the childhood loyalties imposed by genetics and imprinting.*

But why are we here?

Up to now, we have been discussing the immediate origins of our behavioral traits. This is not the usual intent of the question, however, which is, rather: "Where did we come from and what is the *purpose*, or the *meaning* of our existence?"

This is a question often asked; but is it a valid question? Every question is based on an assumption whose validity must be challenged. In this case the assumption is - that there *are* such things as 'purpose' and 'meaning'.

To assign purpose and meaning is a function of mind - not of the insentient universe, so we must ask: "Do these concepts have any reality outside our own minds?"

Our egos demand that we have significance as part of a Grand Scheme which exists far beyond our mundane confines. For this to be true

- it is reasoned - there must be a Grand Intellect in which the Grand Purpose may reside! There is no proof, at present - and probably never will be - that such a mind exists. Yet genes compel many of us *to want* it to be so. Why is this?

The physical and mental characteristics we possess have been selected solely because they have contributed to our success. Any other contributions they might make to our abilities are incidental. Thus, although the means of perception natural selection has equipped us with, allow us to survive in the particular environment in which we evolved, it does not necessarily follow that our senses reveal to us the whole truth of what lies around us. We have already seen how our preconceptions of time, space and cause and effect may be flawed. What then of concepts such as 'purpose' and 'meaning' - are they not simply preconceptions that we possess only because they allow us to plan and to function under the highly specific conditions which exist in our immediate neighborhood - an infinitesimal fraction of the total universe?

Just because we are able to ask a question does not mean that an answer must exist!

Moral Behavior

How would we define **moral behavior**? Of all the infinite number of actions humans are capable of, why do we view certain actions as 'morally correct' and therefore 'desirable'?

To define the term **morality**, let us call upon the main assumption forming the basis of the present thesis - *that human nature has been determined by natural selection since the urges we possess - and ultimately, the goals we seek - have been instilled in us by genes that have survived because the behaviors they induce in us have contributed to our success.*

For the urges we feel to contribute to our success, we must have a powerful 'incentive' to submit to them. We must 'feel' that their reality is beyond question. We must have a 'need' to accept them and a 'fear' of denying them. We must 'want' to believe in their validity and to shun any who would mock or belittle them. We must feel 'good' and 'noble' in yielding to them. We accept these urges as being obvious and natural and therefore we afford them the status of a law, termed by some **natural law**. Thus we feel that in submitting to our natural urges to be 'good' we are 'behaving morally'.

The components of morality

Morality has two main components - **social** and **reproductive.**

Social morality is crucial in our relations with others, since one of the most important goals we pursue is to join and to function successfully in a social group. To do so, we must conduct ourselves within the group in a moral or ethical manner. Thus we may define **social morality** as *treatment of others in our social group in a manner that convinces them to accept us as desirable, beneficial members of the group.*

Reproductive morality is concerned with the creation and protection of our offspring. We have already seen the importance of the proscriptions against incest, homosexuality and pedophilia, and in addition we have aversions to abortion and birth control. The importance of these interdictions is obvious since ignoring them could threaten our genetic succession.

Let us now consider some features of morality that are frequently subject to controversy.

Abortion.

The question as to whether abortion is a sinful or criminal act, arises because of the existence in humans of two powerful emotional drives - the desire for genetic immortality - which treats any threat to the welfare of our offspring with revulsion - and the desires of the ego, or self-interest - one of the most insistent drives in all animals.

The anti-abortionists, upon experiencing their powerful genetically induced abhorrence of the act, are frequently convinced that God is speaking to them, declaring the procedure to be a sin. Their intellect, acting in support of this emotion, provides the knowledge that allows them to be aware of the implications involved, and generates rationalizations in support of their opposition to it. This leads to the declaration (supported by neither fact nor scriptures) that the soul enters the fetus at conception. Although the fetus is obviously not a human at this point, it is a *potential* human possessing a soul, which makes the act in the eyes of the anti-abortionist, a crime of murder.

The intellect also serves those who countenance abortion, making them aware of the consequences of an unwanted birth - the dangers of over population - the possible inconvenience and shame - and provides them with appropriate rationalizations, allowing them to take the 'noble' stance of supporting 'free choice'.

Homosexuality

For the sexual urge to promote reproduction, it must be directed toward members of the opposite sex. So it is, that most individuals experience a revulsion toward sexual activity with those of their own sex. This, no doubt, is a polygenetic characteristic, having a more or less normal distribution in the intensity of this feeling, and hence exhibiting different intensities in each individual. It follows then, that a small percentage of the population will be low in the intensity of their heterosexual drive and some of these will tend toward homosexual behavior.

There is no definite proof that this tendency is genetic, and a frequent argument against this assertion is that, since such behavior would result in homosexuals being devoid of offspring, any genes specifying this behavior would rapidly be eliminated.

On the other hand, there are two arguments which favor retention of genetically based homosexual behavior in the species. The first is that there is no reason for those possessing this proclivity to have a decreased desire to reproduce, and therefore, even though they may find the heterosexual act abhorrent, they will engage in it in the interests of procreation. The second reason is that with an increase in social behavior, a need to conform will have forced homosexuals to seek heterosexual unions.

In spite of these moderating influences, homosexuality tends to reduce reproduction amongst those practicing it, and therefore reduces their ranks in society. This produces a predominately heterosexual society in which an inherent revulsion toward homosexuality becomes the norm. The more ardent heterosexuals regard their strong feelings as revealed knowledge and evidence that God disapproves of this 'unnatural' activity, labeling it a sin, or even a crime. The result is that those experiencing this urge feel guilt and attempt to hide their passions. The best means of proving to themselves and their fellows that they are 'normal' is not to follow their natural urge to form childless unions with others of their own sex, but to avoid social strictures by marrying and having children. The irony of this situation is, that if there is a genetic component to homosexual behavior, those who vociferously oppose it, are, in fact, promoting its retention in the human genome, while on the other hand, tolerance would tend to eliminate it!

Celibacy

Extending the previous arguments to a consideration of the effects to be expected from the practice of celibacy amongst nuns, priests and monks, invites the conclusion that such a custom would inevitably deplete the ranks of the 'godly' within the human genome!

Modesty

As we have seen, it is important for the female to appear to be chaste, modest and faithful to her mate. At the same time, since promiscuity by males within a group would inspire dissension, there is a moral requirement that no male appears to be excessively promiscuous. Furthermore, since a flagrant display of their sexual organs by some members could be construed as an aggressive act - an attempt to divert the affection of the mates of other members - most members of society are restrained by an aversion to exposing themselves to persons of the opposite sex other than their own committed mates. These restraints inspired **sexual modesty**, a trait which in turn led to the wearing of clothes.

As members of *the group* we must prove that we do not posse a threat to the other members. This we do by deferring to them and by resisting the urge to establish superiority over them - bragging about our accomplishments and diminishing their's. Such acts may be classified as **social modesty**.

The Flexibility of Moral Behavior

Natural selection produces individuals whose genetic makeup is peculiar to each. Since moral behavior is instilled by genes, it will not be consistent within the population, but will vary in intensity from individual to individual. Furthermore, it is complex, being composed of a number of traits, such as: affection for, respect for, and empathy with other members of the society. In addition, as we have seen, the ratio of the intensity of our egoistic and altruistic urges also affects our moral behavior and outlook.

These component parts of moral behavior will likely themselves be polygenetic biological traits and as such will vary in intensity amongst individuals within the social group. Thus, if the intensity of each trait could be quantified and the total intensity for each individual calculated, a graph of this sum versus the fraction of the population possessing this intensity, if made in the usual manner, should result in something close to a normal distribution curve. The peak value of this curve would represent the intensity of the compunction to act morally as experienced by the greatest number of individuals in the group, which we may term the *norm*.

On the other hand, most of us find it advantageous at times to dissemble and to attempt to hide our true feelings and even some of our actions. Thus we are not always totally moral. The fact is, however, that *being totally moral does not necessarily promise the highest success rate,* which is why natural selection has adjusted the norm for our moral compunction, not at a maximum value, but rather at a functional optimum, a value that guarantees the greatest success for each of us and our species in a social setting.

In summary...

Our concept of what constitutes moral behavior *is how we would like others to act toward us* and, of course, others desire that we act in the same manner toward them. It should be our purpose, therefore, to convince them that this is the case, and this will be more readily accomplished if we possess a *genuine desire* to do so. This reciprocity generates a conformity of behavior within the society which is established during its social development and becomes fixed in a form to which we refer as the group's 'culture'. But culture remains fixed only so long as the society is not subject to excessive stress, such as war, famine, or even prosperity.

At the same time as we seek conformity, we are constantly being subjected to the demands of our egos, which at times may overcome our altruism. The most successful gene complement, therefore, is one that balances the intensity of these demands at or near a functional optimum.

Thus we must conclude that there is no absolute morality or natural law' - there is only **biological morality** - the **morality of the gene**s - the **morality of expediency** - or, of *what works!*

CHAPTER TEN

FURTHER HUMAN CHARACTERISTICS

In previous chapters we saw how some of the personality traits displayed by humans - including their moral behavior - can have resulted from the operation of selective forces. It is likely that these same forces have given rise to many more human characteristics than those listed above, and it will now be our purpose to consider a few of these.

The Attitudes of Youth

During a tribe's struggle for dominance, it would have been necessary that, as its population increased, it acquired more territory for hunting and food gathering. This would have best been accomplished by a number of smaller groups splintering off the main body of the tribe and locating at some distance from it. To do so safely and effectively, however, a splinter group would have had to be unencumbered by children until the relocation was complete. The ideal time for such migration is obviously just as the members of the group reach puberty, since by then they would have acquired the requisite skills and strength, but will have not yet produced their first offspring.

I would like to suggest that such a mechanism was favored by selection, since it gave an advantage to the tribes in which it operated, and furthermore, that it still functions in today's society, producing what has recently been aptly termed the **generation gap**.

To pursue this idea, let us compare the features that we might reasonably presume such splinter groups to have had, to those we observe in today's teenage youth.

Prior to separation, the members of the departing group would have been encased in a cocoon of parental and tribal discipline from which they would have had to emerge before leaving. Furthermore, such a group would have had to acquire its own discipline and allegiances in opposition to those of the tribe. The splintering would have begun with the development of friendships among small groups of pre-pubertal individuals of the same sex. As these individuals matured, their interests would have begun to include members of groups of the opposite sex with whom they would join. During this period there would have been a transfer of allegiances from the parental society to the forming group, causing a growing irritation with their parents and with other older members of the tribe with whom they previously would have had harmonious relationships.

As the shift in allegiances ran its natural course, there would have been a growing resentment toward the restrictions the older members continued to impose on them and a growing desire to spend more time with their own peers with whom they would have tended to ingratiate themselves. An intense pressure, not only to conform, but to gain status with their cohorts would have grown amongst members of the new group.

In some cases, the established members of the group would have demanded that hopeful recruits undergo initiation or 'hazing' rituals. These would have served two functions. First they would have demonstrated that the initiates were prepared to accept - and submit to - the authority of the group by performing degrading or dangerous acts as demanded by the group. Second, they would have defined the moment at which the transfer of allegiance to the new group took place, thus cementing the new accord. As the group coalesced, a spirited self-assurance would have possessed its members and would have given them the bravado necessary to move into new territory and possibly challenge other tribes.

That these urges are still present in the youth of modern society is evident. Here we note that in a relatively short time at puberty, there is a natural or inherent shift in loyalties - a redefining of the in-group concept - which leads to the formation of juvenile groups. In the slum areas of today's cities with their pressures imposed by high population density, these groups may rapidly become gangs with intense internal loyalties and an aggressive approach to the outside community. With today's mass communications, a new subculture is forged, having its own code of behavior and dress to distinguish it from the encompassing society.

This refocusing is perfectly natural, having contributed to the success of the original gene complex specifying it, but its relatively sudden appearance can be quite disconcerting to the elders, particularly in modern society where migration is seldom a possibility and the lack of other outlets for the young intensifies the resulting conflict. Refocusing proves to be useful, however, to militants and to those dark clerics, who harness the ardor of the young, forming troops or armies by providing the missing outlet in the form of a religious or political 'mission' or 'cause'.

The refocusing appears to be temporary, however, and the original loyalties usually resume, particularly following the arrival of the next generation. In tribal societies, contacts between the parent and satellite communities would usually have been re-established and the tribe, although widened, would still have been intact. On the other hand, if communication was not maintained, the splinter group would probably have evolved slowly into a separate tribe having different language and culture.

In modern society, the aging juvenile groups tend to grow more conservative, with most of their members eventually regaining their original allegiances, especially with the arrival of their own offspring.

No doubt this mechanism was very effective in promoting the spread of dominant variants of our species over the land surface of the earth and must have enhanced their ability to displace other less dominant strains.

Crime

Our view of criminals is that they have betrayed the trust society has placed in them and therefore we have a powerful desire to isolate or eliminate them.   In today's society it is not easy simply to expel transgressors, since no other society will accept them. Instead, criminals are isolated from society in prisons, penal colonies or penitentiaries. For the most serious crimes, there are always those amongst us who, driven by anger when confronted by the treacherous actions of the criminal, demand the death penalty.

There are a variety of motivations for criminal behavior, but I would like to consider two types in particular.

The Gang Member

First let us consider the motivations that drive the gang member. This is usually an individual who has transferred his allegiance completely from society at large to the gang. His reasons for doing so may vary but it is usually the result of alienation from the mainstream society, perhaps because of his youth, as mentioned above, or because he has been denied access to the benefits of society that he sees others enjoying. In either case he feels society has excluded and therefore betrayed him. The gang becomes his focus and his actions towards its members, his moral imperative. Although he may feel no compunction about lying to, stealing from, injuring or even killing those who are not gang members, he would not consider taking such actions against his comrades unless they themselves should prove to be disloyal toward him. Gaining respect within the gang becomes his main motivation, and he will perform almost any act to earn the commendation of his confreres. He may be just as altruistic as any member of any other group, sacrificing his welfare for that of the others - the only difference being that the gang, and not society at large, provides a focus for his loyalty. Youth groups, churches and other religious and political organizations can deflect prospective gang members by providing those who feel that they have been rejected or betrayed by society with an alternate refuge, where they can enjoy acceptance and self respect.

The Solitary Criminal

The second type of criminal motivation that I would like to consider drives those whose actions are solitary. The main characteristic of this type of criminal is that the intensity of his altruistic feelings is low or absent while that of his egoism is high. If we had a measure of altruism, we would probably find that his index for this quality was located in the lower fringe or tail of the distribution curve for the populace at large. Thus he is a member of a very small portion of the population, consisting of those who are ruled almost entirely by their egos. He feels no empathy with, nor sympathy for others, whom, on the contrary, he considers as objects to be used for his own pleasure or profit. He learns to curb or hide his appetites for fear of reprisals and will only attempt to satiate them when he feels he will not be discovered doing so. Remorse for his actions is minimal or absent. Sadistic murder and sex crimes are his specialty, but society finds the most heinous of his crimes to be those perpetrated against children - as, for example by the pedophile - since such acts threaten the gene succession of the other members directly and therefore have an intensely negative connotation in their minds.

While such criminals are considered to be pathological, their actions are driven by normal genetic forces - they are simply seeking the goals provided for them by their genetic makeup. In this they are normal. It is the goals they seek that differ from the norm. Society, however, must protect itself from any harm that such behavior might inflict on it and so it is incumbent upon those of outlying motivations, to curb their divergent cravings - or suffer the wrath of society! The suggestion that such deviant behavior can be 'cured' is as misguided as suggesting that shortness of stature can be 'cured', as both are inerrant characteristics of these individuals.

Skin Color

There are several theories as to why initially the light-skin races seem to locate in the northern regions of the earth while those with darker skin are found in the tropical regions. Perhaps the most common explanation contends that since vitamin D is synthesized by the body using light incident on the skin, more intense light is required by those having darker skin and as a result, such persons will have, in the past, tended to suffer from a deficiency of this vitamin at higher latitudes. On the other hand, those individuals lacking pigment suffer skin damage under the intense sunlight of the tropical regions. Whatever the reason, it appears that, other factors being equal, individuals thrive and are therefore more comfortable at latitudes where the intensity of sunlight is inverse to the intensity of their skin pigmentation.

The degree of skin pigmentation, like most biological features, is genetically determined and therefore statistical in nature, which means that in any population there will be some individuals with darker and some with lighter skin than average. As a consequence, one can expect a certain refluxing of the genes for skin color. In the case of Africa and Europe, for example, whatever the origin of their populations, over the millennia, gene refluxing, driven by migration, would have tended to concentrate gene complexes specifying skin pigmentation in the south, while their alleles for light skin would be concentrated toward the north, and as a result of this process, the average individual tends to locate in the region to which she or he is best suited.

Humor

Many animals display what might be termed an **assembly call**. This has the same function as the alarm call since through it *an animal perceiving danger alerts other members of its group*. The alarm call generally incites the members of the group to flight. The **assembly call,** on the other hand, *promotes the gathering of the group in one location.* Barking and howling encourages canines to assemble for the purpose of forming a hunting pack. The hooting of apes causes the assembly of the troop to confront a rival group or an intruder.

The assembly call has two important features. Firstly it compels those hearing it to repeat it. Thus when one dog hears others barking, it experiences an almost irresistible urge to join in. So too with many birds, such as crows that assemble to drive away an owl, each joins in the cacophony raised by the others. The advantage gained by an irresistible urge to repeat the call is, obviously, that it guarantees that the call reaches all members of the group.

Second, the assembly call promotes the cohesiveness of the group, since on hearing it, all members experience a powerful urge not only to assemble, but to be prepared to confront an opponent. Thus, it increases the binding of the in-group by stressing the existence of an out-group.

I would like to suggest that **laughter** is the **human assembly call,** possibly having the same genetic origin as the hooting of the great apes. We are all aware of the urge to join a group of laughing individuals and of the 'infectious' nature that group laughter displays amongst members of a group, causing them all to join in. In fact laughter is seldom as enjoyable to a lone individual as it is to the same individual in a group or audience.

Humor can be highly effective in defining the group, due to the fact that humorous stories frequently have as a butt, or object, one who is not a member of the group sharing the story, but rather is the one held up for ridicule by the group. Thus we have racial, national, religious, political, and social jokes that play on and accentuate, or even exaggerate by 'aping', the differences between the audience (the in-group) and the individual or group portrayed as the object of ridicule (the out-group).

The survival value of humor is that it binds the group, promoting camaraderie amongst its members. This is the reason it has a positive connotation and why we find it enjoyable. Since the object of humor is usually not considered to be a member of the group, it is usually frightening and therefore unpleasant to be caste as such and we may react with anger at the betrayal of any who portray us in this way. Thus we find ridicule or 'being laughed at' offensive, or even frightening.

The person who relates a humorous story, on the other hand, gives pleasure to his audience and is generally admired. As raconteur, one can caste oneself as the butt, thus displaying modesty and a willingness to humble oneself before the group. Such an act may also reduce the perception others may have of us as a possible threat, particularly upon a first meeting. Deciding whether others are a threat to us is an extremely important aspect of our social interactions as humans. It is our skeptical nature that compels us to make such decisions.

We perceive threatening persons to be those who would harm us (or our loved ones) physically or socially, while those who we are sure would not do so, are those whom we count as our friends. As we do not view either children or friends as a threat, we find that observing their small foibles gives us pleasure and endears them to us.

CHAPTER ELEVEN

SUMMARY

Insistent nature doth us bind,
To seek the shining prize.
Possessing it at last, we find,
But dims it in our eyes!

'Tis then we seek another goal,
More distant than the first,
For life, it seems, besets us with,
An ache of constant thirst!

The Theory of Evolution states that *all life forms on earth have evolved from simpler forms, starting with an initial self-replicating system that arose naturally some three to three and a half billion years ago.* The changes that have occurred during this period were driven by **natural selection**, which is itself no more than the preservation of **successful individuals** - *those whose offspring reproduce* and who thereby forge a link in the chain of life. This mechanism is essentially simple, but by functioning in concert with mutation, its consequences are profound. Together, these mechanisms have produced an immense variety of life forms.

Every species is defined by the characteristics, or traits, that it inherits from its parents. These define the physical structure of each individual, and in animals, contribute to their behavior as well. **Behavior, in turn, *results from the functioning of the mind which makes decisions as to the next activity the animal is to undertake.***

As humans, we are proud of our rational powers, which, we observe, exceed that of all other animals. Because of this, we are convinced that our actions are directed more by reason, than by the instincts and emotions that motivate lesser animals. The truth is, however, that we are driven by many of the same forces that drive all animals, and moreover, without these drives we would simply not function at all!

Reasoning is a relative process that must start with a premise or initial assumption. Thus, given the premise: "I *want* to survive," reasoning leads us to the conclusions: "therefore I must eat" and "therefore I must avoid danger." The latter conclusion, in turn, leads to the further deduction: "therefore I must join others of my own kind for protection." These are vital decisions, which no amount of reasoning could render, unless provided by initial premises!

Since reasoning cannot provide its own premises, these must be furnished by genes whose continued propagation depends on the degree to which the goals (or premises) they instill contribute to the success of their carrier. Our minds, then, appear to have two distinct components: the first, which we may term the emotional mind, provides the goals, the desires and the wants, that become the premises upon which, the second component, the rational mind, performs its functions. The genes also provide the individual with the physical capabilities it requires to attain the goals it seeks, in the form of a mobile body.

Although all animals seek the goals implicit in their own survival, it is only we humans who seek a **purpose** for this activity, driven as we are by an ego that insists that our lives must have *significance*, since the goals we seek are *noble*! But there are no 'noble' goals - only those prosaic, but essential, aims instilled in all of us by our genes!

As I have maintained throughout, an animal may, on most occasions, be directed by reason to pursue those activities that promote its welfare - but it is more likely that it will do so consistently if it possesses an innate desire to act in a beneficial manner. We may conclude then, that human behavior is based on inherited tendencies moderated by expediency - as perceived by the intellect - and that we are driven to act in certain ways by forces we occasionally find mysterious, but which are, in fact, determined by our genetic make-up. Once again I insist that our goals are not intellectually generated, but are the expressions of inherent desires that have, on the average during human evolution, proven to be advantageous to those individuals possessing them and hence to the gene complexes specifying them.

It was suggested above that our thinking is essentially conceptual and that concepts form the building blocks of our minds. Learning consists of accumulating new information provided by the senses, which is then combined with older, more familiar notions, to form new concepts.

It was also suggested that conceptual thinking makes speech possible, since speaking consists of giving nomenclature to our concepts which are then transmitted by sound to other individuals whose conceptual nomenclature is similar to ours.

Personalities

As a result of its evolutionary history, the human population contains a rich mix of genes specifying behavioral traits. These include genes not only ranging from those most prominent in the agrarian, to those specifying the hunter-gatherer mentality, but also those responsible for the usual religious, gregarious, selfish, skeptical, conservative, altruistic and nonconformist traits, as well as such minor traits as curiosity, humor, industriousness, etc. Furthermore, some humans are subject to bizarre and unaccountable urges resulting in, what others consider to be, "eccentric" or "peculiar" behavior. These may result either from normal urges expressed in single individuals with an excessively high or low intensity, or from unusual urges that have arisen in the past due to the chance occurrence of minor mutations. Such traits, which would be unlikely to confer either a large advantage or disadvantage on the individual, would have been neither eliminated nor favored by natural selection and would therefore be present at a low frequency in the general populace. All these traits, combined with a range of mental capacities, personal history and exposure to environmental factors, provide the almost limitless and fascinating variety of personalities that modern humans display! In fact the variation in personalities is probably as great as that in physical appearance (which is also under genetic control) and, as a result, we seldom find any two individuals who are identical in appearance - or personality.

Happiness

We are generally happiest - and most relaxed - when yielding to our natural urges. Thus, the fortunate are those whose urges direct them to act in the most socially acceptable manner. For these people, being 'good' is accomplished with ease and we think of them as 'gracious'. Their good fortune is similar to that of those whose physical appearance, by chance, corresponds closely to the universal preconception of 'beauty'. Such people are generally deferred to, and move easily to the center of the herd - the position of greatest security. For others, such a position must be contested, and for them an 'aggressive' or 'competitive' nature is advantageous.

Our desires drive us constantly, their relentless nature stemming from the fact that there would be no selective advantage to any animal that did not persist in its attempts to advance itself. Having attained one goal we seek another, which is why humans are, in fact, ill designed for leisure. We do not ask for freedom from our longings but for **the power to fulfill them,** which we equate with **happiness**.

Few if any of us have the ability to attain our goals, but biological success does not only come from *reaching* our goals, but rather, from *attempting* to do so.

To live is to strive. Thus it is that we are forever doomed to seek the shining prize!

EPILOGUE

We are all here by chance - egos contending with egos;
hard skeletal selves, sheathed in the soft seemly flesh of goodness;
driven by the lash of pain and the lure of pleasure
to do the genes' mindless bidding!

"So," you might ask, "if all you say is true, what is left? Do we have no real mastery over our own actions but are simply slaves to our genes? Are the qualities of goodness and nobility illusions? Is there no loving God Who nurtures us and Whose great purpose we are here to fulfill? Is the God we worship no more than a lie told by our genes? Is our existence a mere scintillation in the black night of eternity? Are we destined forever to be imprisoned in this precarious interface between absolute cold and boundless heat - the minuscule and the immense - the infinite past and inscrutable eternity?"

Such thoughts are uncomfortable and not acceptable to most of us. The majority of humans believe what they want to believe - what they find to be most reassuring - or what their genes make them *want* to believe.

Unfortunately, however, *palatability is not a criterion for credibility!*

On the other hand, one might ask: "Does our welfare depend on our believing in lies?" I prefer to think not!

How then are we to face our existence knowing we are alone? Our first task is to assess the true nature of our being. Viewing the universe in which we live, we are appalled by its size, its age, its terrible cataclysmic possibilities! In comparison we are small, fleeting, and impotent. Are we therefore insignificant?

No!

Although we have occupied an insignificant locale trapped in this tenuous global membrane, each of us is a microcosm of incredible intricacy. We are all heirs to evolutionary wisdom, which has been enriched throughout three and a half billion years of rejecting the crude in favor of the elegant. As a result, each of us is possessed of a living body, which, despite its mundane origins, is a machine of exquisite complexity - containing a brain composed of 1,400 grams of what is, in all probability, the most highly complex material (gram for gram) of any in the universe. Nowhere is there likely to be such a store of information - such a degree of improbability. In this regard, living organisms tower above all else in the universe! Life is an entropy trough of profound depth - a pinnacle of order rising from a vast sea of tempestuous disorder!

Although the cosmos is paramount in size, age and power, we exceed all in complexity and in the ability to generate thoughts!

But if we are not part of a cosmic plan, are we therefore aimless - without purpose or meaning?

No!

Our purpose - wrought by chance - is to exploit life, the precious treasure each of us has to enjoy; to create the civilization all of us desire; to build a mansion in which the future may dwell. Each life adds one building block to this structure; some blocks are large, some small; some plain, some ornate; some are ugly and misshapen, threatening the integrity of the structure, while a few form the very lintels and keystones crucial to design.

Some fashion structures for support - others the doors and windows of enlightenment; some are mere grains of sand in the mortar securing the walls, but ***all contribute, and the purpose of all is to build the splendid edifice of human achievement!***

Surely this is a noble goal!

Surely this gives meaning to us all!

In our short sojourn, we have accumulated a vast store of knowledge and of aesthetic treasures. Each generation adds to this bounty. The promise for the future is boundless!

Forced as we are to function in a world with no absolutes, we must establish our own standards. Let us therefore adopt the **humanist maxim** that: *"Mankind is the measure of all things."* Let us revel in our humanity! Let us accept the grander, nobler goals that chance has charged us with!

The inevitable demise of the cosmos - either through endless expansion and thermodynamic death - or a grinding halt to space and time - is quoted by some as a reason for despair. Such events will not occur for many billions of years, however, leaving us with a future, which, by our standards, is virtually infinite. Life has only recently emerged from its primordial ooze, but now stands proudly erect facing a dawn of immense promise. Eons of adventure lie before us - the journey has just begun!

We now stand on the shores of a vast continent - the continent of the mind - that is open to our conquest. But first, we must understand and free ourselves, casting off the bonds of our own illusions. We must accept that the world in which we now live is not the one in which we evolved, and that therefore, the goals and emotions that brought us to our present dominant state are not necessarily valid today. We are no longer - as were our ancestors - ignorant beasts responding blindly to our inherent urges, but intelligent beings, who, while subject to the same urges, are aware of the consequences of our actions. We cannot ignore the responsibility that such knowledge bestows!

We have virtually stemmed the flow of death amongst the young - but not the flow of life. The forces that once stabilized our numbers have been thwarted - *but only temporarily*. The laws of nature are inexorable.

It is *we* who must accommodate - not *they*! If we do not limit our numbers voluntarily, nature will impose her own limits - without mercy!

The accelerating and unnatural rise in population of our species has become the gravest and most urgent problem we face. The human race is rapidly becoming a dangerous pollutant in the biosphere. So serious is this problem, that we must accept that couples who conceive children for whom they are unable to provide are *both* guilty of a crime against humanity - and nature. Furthermore, those who support or encourage such acts must bear the responsibility for the inevitable tragedy that an unfettered birthrate is sure to provoke. The technical means of pursuing responsible parenthood - *without resorting to the repulsive act of abortion* - are available and should be provided to all.

The argument that artificial birth control is unnatural while the 'rhythm method' is not, is a fallacy. As we have seen, intercourse between parents serves a 'natural' double function - not least of which is to cement the parental union in the interests of the family and the security of the children. To insist that fear of unwanted pregnancy be companion to such acts of love, is to subvert this function.

The urge to promote the welfare of one's immediate group at the expense of the rest is no longer appropriate. While it may have served to establish *Homo sapiens* in the past, any sizable conflict within the species now, could destroy it. The true humanist views the entire species as within her or his moral domain. Each individual has a contribution to make; each deserves to enjoy her or his own self-respect. Our very survival as a species depends on the universal acceptance of these simple facts!

Homo sapiens, during its short span, has demonstrated an appalling power for both good and evil; we must wield that power for good - not for one faction - but for all!

Should we succeed in stabilizing our global population and in eliminating conflict, there need be no time limit to our habitation of the planet. Our species could well continue to flourish for hundreds of thousands of years into the future - barring only a major catastrophic event!

Such a prolonged tenure would, of course, require a virtually endless supply of energy and this could only be obtained from one source - the sun, whose beneficence we must learn to exploit. In the meantime, we will continue to deplete the planet's fossil fuels, and ultimately its nuclear materials as well. All available mineral resources would eventually be mined but could subsequently be recycled as required in the manufacture of new products. By a judicious regulation of the population, a stable food supply could be established which would in turn stabilize the carbon cycle, freeing us from the drastic effects of a changing atmospheric and oceanic carbon dioxide concentration.

* * * * *

There are no criteria that we may utilize to justify our desire for the immortality of our species. There is only the desire itself - the ultimate **emotional imperative!**

* * * * *

The forces that brought us to our present dominance have burdened us with awesome powers. We must therefore ask ourselves:

- will the embers of life, inflamed by a tiny spark billions of years ago, continue to glow with a steadily increasing brilliance throughout future eons?
- or will they be consumed in one final flash of folly?
- or will they slowly die, smothered in their own foul fumes?

The reins of life are in our hands - the course is ours to choose! Let us, therefore, choose to exalt the nobler aspirations of mankind intelligently - eschewing blind emotion!

INDEX

Terms printed in boldface are defined in the text. The pages on which these definitions occur, are also presented in boldface.

INDEX